Animals of the Soul

The author with Black Elk.

Animals of the Soul
Sacred Animals of the Oglala Sioux

Joseph Epes Brown

ELEMENT
Rockport, Massachusetts ● Shaftesbury, Dorset

© 1992 Joseph Epes Brown

Published in the USA in 1992 by
Element, Inc.
42 Broadway, Rockport, MA 01966

Published in Great Britain in 1992 by
Element Books Limited
Longmead, Shaftesbury, Dorset

The photographs and drawings appearing on pages 5, 24, 26, 28, 31, 36,
41, 53, 58, 73, 78, 86, 92, and 117 are courtesy of the Smithsonian
Institution. The National Museum of Canada located in Ottawa, Ontario
supplied the photographs on pages 50 and 112. Except where noted, all
other photographs and drawings are the property of Joseph Epes Brown.

Text design by Nancy Lawrence
Phototypeset by Intype, London
Cover illustration by Martin Red Bear
Cover design by Max Fairbrother
Printed in the United States of America by
Edwards Brothers, Inc.

Library of Congress Cataloging-in-Publication Data

Brown, Joseph Epes.
Animals of the soul: Sacred Animals of the Oglala Sioux
Joseph Epes Brown.
Includes bibliographical references.
1. Oglala Indians—Folklore. 2. Oglala Indians—Religion and
mythology. 3. Oglala Indians—Rites and ceremonies. 4. Bestiaries.
5. Animals—Great Plains—Folklore. I. Title.
E99 03B76 1991   398.2'089975—dc20   91–29083

British Library Cataloguing in Publication Data

Brown, Joseph Epes
Animals of the soul: Sacred Animals of the Oglala Souix.
I. Title
299.78

ISBN 1–85230–343–3 paperback
ISBN 1–85230–297–6 hardback

Table of Contents

Foreword

This remarkable book stands as a testament to the author's lifelong commitment to the Oglala Sioux. The seeds of Joseph Brown's interest in the Native American experience were sown in Maine where he grew up and made friends with the Wabaniki who taught him to hunt and fish. After World War II, he read Neihardt's *Black Elk Speaks*, which was the story of a young Oglala Sioux's visions and his subsequent years as a medicine man during the wars of the late nineteenth century which intensified the suffering of Native Americans and brought to an end their basic way of life.

Neihardt's book had a profound effect on the young Joseph Brown, and when he heard that Black Elk was still alive, he bought an old Ford truck, built a home for himself in the back, and set off to track him down. After searching for four months, he found him in Nebraska with a band of Oglalas who were working in the potato fields. They were living in canvas-wall tents, and as he had been instructed, Joseph hit the outside of Black Elk's tent – a custom dating back to the old tepee days. When he entered, Black Elk, who was nearly blind, looked up and said, "Well, it's about time you came. I've been waiting for you. What took you so long?" Thus began their long friendship. Joseph picked potatoes with the near-starving family during that very cold winter, and when they later returned home to Manderson, North Dakota, he went too and lived with them for several years. During this time he hunted and fished with them and listened while Black Elk passed on to him the teachings of the sacred rites of the Oglala, which were later to be published under the title *The Sacred Pipe*.

Joseph still remembers an occasion one winter during this period when game was scarce, and Black Elk's large family had become desperately hungry. Sitting on a bluff with no game in sight, he began singing a song Black Elk had taught him – a song for bringing in the animals. After several minutes of singing, a herd of deer appeared. Everyone ate well that night!

Among many other things, Joseph was taught the correct way of smoking the pipe. He was shown how to smoke it in preparation for the hunt, and was taught how to make an offering after the hunt by blowing the smoke into the nostrils of the dead animal, a ritual way of thanking the creature for giving its life.

Since Joseph had a truck, he was frequently asked to take the Black Elk family on trips. On one such, to Denver, he was accompanied by Black Elk himself. After several unsuccessful attempts to find a hotel that would accommodate Indians, they finally found a seedy place in a very run-down area. Upon entering the room, Black Elk said, "I sure feel dirty here in this city. We must have a Sweat and get clean!" Whereupon he proceeded to prepare a Sweat right there in the middle of the hotel room using a blanket, a table, and a panful of coals.

During this period, Joseph also became intimate with the great Native American leaders of the era, including Little Warrior, a close friend of Black Elk and a noted Shaman, and he remained with Black Elk and his family until the Lakota visionary's death in 1950. He then returned east to write *The Sacred Pipe*, which he did during a harsh Maine winter while living in a small one-room cabin with his new Swiss wife, Elenita.

After completing the book, Joseph resumed the academic career which he had begun years earlier at Bowdoin College in Maine and continued later at Haverford College in Pennsylvania. He very much wanted the field of Native American studies to have its rightful place within university curricula and, knowing it to be necessary for his work, he began a Master's degree in Anthropology. However, he came into conflict with the school over such issues as the desecration of burial grounds by those anthropologists who saw the indigenous peoples as inferior. So for several years he turned his back on his promising anthropological career at the university to undertake a more profoundly religious training in American Indian scholarship with the Swedish religious historian, Ake Hultkrantz. It was during this period in Stockholm that he researched and wrote his animal thesis which is the premise for this book.

There followed a brief teaching stay at Indiana University where he pioneered the first Native American Studies program, before returning to the west where he could be nearer to the indigenous peoples so close to his heart. With a caravan of trucks and two horse trailers, he and his wife and their four children moved to the open spaces of Montana, and to the University of Montana where he has taught for over twenty years.

There he built a home and a horse ranch, which he works with family members. He is happiest surrounded by his family, the animals, the land, doing good hard work, while his classes at the University have been an inspiration to countless students who, as he says, "keep me straight." One such student remembers an occasion when he arrived late for class, still wearing his work clothes, cowboy hat, and boots. "Forgive me," he said, "I had to chase my stampeding buffalo out of a neighbor lady's arbor vitae!"

It is important for the reader to recognize that, in addition to the doctoral thesis mentioned above, this volume is made up of numerous articles published by Dr Brown during his very long career. This has resulted in occasional shifts in diction and tone, and, inevitably, in some repetition. But these are minor concerns which simply reflect the different eras and experiences of the author's life. They in no way detract from the book's central theme – the relationships between a culture and its animal relatives. It is this focus which gives the individual sections of the book their essential cohesion and unity.

Central to this spiritual relationship between the native peoples and the animals of their environment is the vision quest. In this ritual, the initiate seeks the wisdom and guidance of an animal helper, guardian, or teacher. Although the quest takes place in "this world," it is not limited by a materialistic sense of time and space. The quest is a ritual entry into sacred time and space. It recreates a unified experience of time and eternity, nature and supernature, of first and present creation. Our sacred texts depict relations between animals and humans in the Eden of first creation as having been more intimate and fluid. In that time and place, transformations occurred naturally between creature and creature, between creature and Creator. And it was a time and place where these transformations were expressed artfully in a language of dreams and visionary forms. The vision quest recreates the paradise experience, not just through events of the past, but within the spontaneous moments of our present lives.

Some years ago in Canada, Joseph Brown gave a talk in which he focused on the vision quest as a resource for all of us. His words speak for themselves:

> . . . The vision quest must always be preceded by rites of purification through the use of the sweat lodge. Here the novice is helped to enter into the necessary state of humility, to undergo, as it were, a spiritual rebirth. The person also, through rites and prayers, and through the form and materials of the lodge itself, is aided in establishing relationships with the primary elements, earth, air, fire, and water, and with all the beings of the earth, the animals, the winged creatures, and all that grows from the earth. Such relationships additionally are strengthened in these rites of purification through the use of a sacred pipe, the communal and sacramental smoking of which establishes a ritual relationship with all of creation and with the very source of life.
>
> The quest itself must be undertaken in solitude and in silence upon a mountain, or some isolated place well away from the camp. The seeker's state of concentration is aided through the delineation of a protecting sacred area within which the person must remain and move about only in accord with prescribed ritual patterns, usually defined by the four directions of space in their relation to an established center. One must always be attentive and listen, for it is believed that the sacred powers may manifest themselves through any form or being of the natural world, which may appear visually or which may wish to communicate through some audible message. The presence and word of the Great Mystery is within every being, every thing, every event. Even the smallest being, a little ant for example, may appear and communicate something of the power of the Great Mystery that is behind all forms of creation.

The powers and beings of the world wish to communicate with man; they wish to establish a relationship, but may only do so where the recipient is in a state of humility, and is attentive with all his being. Since such humility is fostered through sacrifice, the seeker must neither eat nor drink for the duration of his quest, often three or four days. Being there alone and almost naked, he will realize the force of the elements through exposure and suffering.

It has been said by many that the greatest support in the quest, and in the course of life itself, is silence, for ultimately silence is the very voice of the Great Mystery. The man or woman, however, is also enjoined to pray, indeed to pray continually, either silently, in an audible voice, or through song. The old Lakota sage, Black Elk, once told me of a prayer he often repeated continually during his quests. It was simply: "Grandfather, Great Spirit, have pity on me." In prayer, he also said, one should express thankfulness, gratitude, for all those gifts which are upon and above this earth.

. . . Contemporary confusions concerning the prerequisite conditions for true spiritual realization abound in the world today. This is eminently comprehensible and evident to many. We live under the forces of a pervasive, materialistic outlook, spreading essentially from the Western world. This outlook is causally related to the erosion of the great spiritual legacies of this world. Humankind has become increasingly a prisoner of the limits of its vision and the manner in which it experiences the world. In seeking release from this constricting experience of a continually changing physical multiplicity, and motivated by a nostalgia for a lost more real world of true freedom, many have turned in every possible direction for alternative answers. Due, however, to the erosion and spiritual impoverishment of one's own proper tradition, or rather, due to our inability in these times to understand the true nature of these traditions, there is left no real criteria for discrimination, evaluation, and eventual choice rooted in true knowledge. In addition, there is the problem that motivation in the quest, often undertaken with the greatest sincerity, may actually be, through the self-will of the ego, sentimentality, or the desire, self-defeating in itself, for some otherworldly, liberating mystical experience which nevertheless still appears within the realm of limiting phenomena. Under such conditions there is no guarantee that what is found will not lead to further frustrations, and often, as is the case with altered states of consciousness through the use of drugs, to a sinking within the lower chaotic depth of one's being, and thus to a deepening intensification of the original problem.

. . . One explanation for the current new willingness to understand Native Americans and their lifeways is the fact that, being rooted in American land for thousands of years, the Indians' otherwise very diverse cultures have all come to express rich spiritual relationships with this American land; indeed the forms and symbols bearing these values are all drawn from the details of each people's particular geographic environment. Many Native Americans still live what one might call a metaphysics of nature, spelled out by each group in great detail, and defining responsibilities and the true nature of that vast web of man's cyclical interrelationships with the elements, the earth, and all that lives upon this land. The echoes of such a message have caught the attention of at least a few within a society that finally has been forced by hard circumstances to recognize the gravity of our ecological crisis, and thus, to seek answers that speak to root causes rather than continually treating the ever-recurring symptoms of the problem.

In *Animals of the Soul*, Joseph Brown offers us the assurance that, even in this apparently uninspiring age, there is the ever-present potential for a return to the Spirit.

Introduction

Let a man decide upon his favorite animal and make a study of it—let him learn to understand its sounds and motions. The animals want to communicate with man, but Wakan-Tanka *does not intend they shall do so directly—man must do the greater part in securing an understanding.*
                              —Brave Buffalo, Standing Rock[1]

You ought to follow the example of shunk-tokecha *(wolf). Even when he is surprised and runs for his life, he will pause to take one more look at you before he enters his final retreat. So you must take a second look at everything you see.*   —Ohiyesa[2]

Goats are very mysterious, as they walk on cliffs and other high places; and those who dream of goats or have revelations from them imitate their actions. Such men can find their way up and down cliffs, the rocks get soft under their feet, enabling them to maintain a foothold, but they close up behind them, leaving no trace.
                              —from the Teton Sioux[3]

The swallow's flying precedes a thunderstorm. This bird is closely related to the thunderbird. The action of a swallow is very agile. The greatest aid to a warrior is a good horse, and what a warrior desires most for his horse is that it may be as swift as the swallow in dodging the enemy or in direct flight.   —Lone Man[4]

Each animal has its own Master Spirit which owns all the animals of its kind . . . so all the animals are the children of the Master Spirit that owns them. It is just like a large family.   —Raining Bird (Cree)[5]

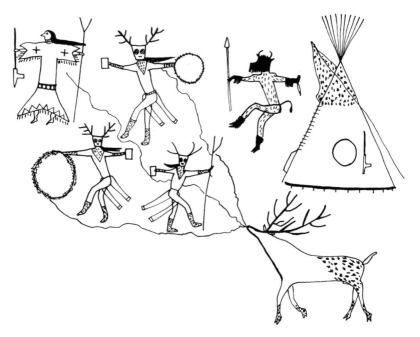

To man as a hunter, the divine became transparent above all in the animals.   —Ivar Paulson

An intense interaction necessarily takes place between the people of a nomadic hunting culture and the animals of their habitat. This is evidenced in a rich variety of cultural expressions, which projects what could be called the people's total worldview. The Oglala Sioux of the North American Plains are a classic example of such a culture. In the words of one of them, Brave Buffalo of Standing Rock, "When I was ten years of age I looked at the land and the rivers, the sky above and the animals around me, and could not fail to realize that they were made by some great Power. I was so anxious to understand this Power that I questioned the trees and the bushes."[1]

The Sacred Power of Animals

What precisely is the Oglala's conception of "power" as manifested through the animals? What is the relationship between the multiplicity of such "powers" and a unitary concept of a "Supreme Being"? Who, or what, is the Indian's acquired "guardian spirit," and what is the relationship between this "spirit power" and the "master" of all the animals?

Basic to the Plains Indians' culture was the vision quest, the search for the power and protection of a tutelary spirit. Among the Oglala, for whom it was termed "crying for a vision," the quest was participated in by virtually all the men and, although less frequently and in a somewhat less rigorous form, often also by women. "Every man can cry for a vision, or 'lament,' " Black Elk told me, "and in the old days we all — men and women — lamented all the time." Although the quest which resulted in the attainment of a vision need not necessarily involve formal acquisition of a "guardian spirit," normally the successful encounter was with a bird or an animal. It was through this agency that the desired goal, or even quality of being, could be achieved if the seeker then carried out properly the specific instructions which were conveyed to him by his mentor.

Dreams and the Vision Quest

For the Oglala it seems that distinguishing between dream and vision is of little or no concern, for many of the recorded encounters with animal spirits which took place in the dream state held the same "power" as if the experience had been a waking vision. I remember the emotion and intensity with which Black Elk described a dream to me one morning: "I was taken away from this world into a vast tipi, which seemed to be as large as the world itself, and painted on the inside were every kind of four-legged being, winged-being, and all the crawling peoples. The peoples that were there in that lodge, they talked to me, just as I am talking to you."

Evidently in both dream and vision there is an intensification of the interrelationships with animal forms, and these experiences go beyond and are deeper than the encounters which take place in the waking state. There is a shift to another level of cognition, on which the Oglala is no longer encountering the phenomenal animal, but rather archetypal "essences" appearing in animal forms. Although these could appear in

almost any of the forms of the natural world, in an overwhelming majority of documented cases the vision encounter was
with representatives of a wide range of animals and birds, any
of which could become the seeker's "guardian spirit." After
the quest, the "lamenter" returns to his sponsor who interprets
the vision, and instructs the man as to actions which must be
taken to "actualize" the power he has received.

The component elements of either the dream or vision in
which the animals or birds appear may take a number of forms.
Among the recurring patterns are association of the animal or
bird "spirit-form" with the powers of the four directions, which
appear in conjunction with manifestations of the terrifying
aspects of these powers, notably the Thunder-Beings. (The
vision quests normally take place between early spring and fall
when thunderstorms are the most frequent and violent in the
Plains.) Or men may turn into animals, and vice versa, or one
species of animal may shift into another, or an animal may
take on some plant form which is to become the sacred medicinal herb later identified and used in curing. Frequently it is
the animal who finally disappears who becomes the seeker's
guardian spirit; or else, ". . . the animal that appeared . . .
entered his body and became part of his *wakan* strength. He
might fast many times and have many such tutelary spirits
within his body."[2]

It is interesting to note that though all men were expected
to seek through a vision a "tutelary spirit," certainly not all
received such favor, and among those that did there were great
variations in its quality. For some, experiences were of such
an intense and recurring nature that the recipient might
become one of a number of types of "medicine men"; those
who dreamed or had visions of the Thunder-Beings or of dogs
were destined to become *hehoka*, or contraries. Although the
Oglala rarely express it explicitly, and never systematically,
there is a certain ranking of the animals, or of their underlying
"spirit-power." Grizzly Bear, for example, was understood to
be chief of the underground earth forces, conceived in a negative and terrifying aspect; the bison was chief, in an exclusively
positive sense, over all animals of the surface of the earth, and
the eagle was seen to have supremacy over all the flying
beings. Some animals outranked others in terms of their

A wooden turtle spoon.

"attracting" powers, and the spider outranked all in terms of cleverness. So it may be said that the Oglala's conception of his guardian animal spirits represents *qualitatively* different manifestations of power, which may be obtained by men under certain conditions.

Success in the vision quest brought with it certain obligations. Among other things (such as the making of a fetish or a medicine bundle) the one who had received a vision was normally obliged, especially in the case of a powerful experience, to extend and share it by enacting it in some way, sometimes by a dance ceremonial, or by singing the songs learned in the vision, or in some other form. By dynamically acting out or dancing the inner, subjective experience, a reintensification of it results, and the larger social group is able to participate. This helps to influence the young people toward this quality of experience and so to preserve the central values.

A detailed account of one such dance ceremonial – Black Elk's "Horse Dance" – can be found on p. 66. In that instance, the ritual enactment of the vision was so close to the original experience that the vision itself recurred to Black Elk: ". . .

what we then were doing," he said "was like a shadow cast upon the earth from yonder vision in the heavens, so bright it was and clear. I knew the real was yonder and the darkened dream of it was here."

A Worldview

Evidence such as this indicates that the gradations of reality which the Oglala attribute to the components of this world represent a type of thinking, an attitude of mind, which is very different from that of the non-Indian. We find here an experienced world which sets less rigid limits than those obtaining for the non-Indian. There is a fluidity and transparency to their apperceptions of the phenomenal world which permits no absolute line to be drawn, for example, between the worlds of animals, men, or spirits. I could cite numerous parallels from Black Elk's own lips to this statement of his quoted by Neihardt: "Crazy Horse dreamed and went into the world where there is nothing but the spirits of all things. That is the real world that is behind this one, and everything we see here is something like a shadow from that world." Sword, another great Oglala medicine man, told James Walker that "the Four Winds is an immaterial god, whose substance is never visible. . . . While he is one god, he is four individuals. . . . The word *Wakan-Tanka* means all the *wakan* beings because they are all as if one."[3]

To the non-Indian, the Oglala world structure, modes of

classification, and associative processes often appear incomprehensible; but the world of the Lakota is neither unstructured nor chaotic, for underlying the fluidity of appearances there is the binding thread of the *wakan* concept, and an ultimate coalescence of the multiple into the unifying principle of *Wakan-Tanka*, whose multiplicity of aspects does not compromise an essential unity. Such seemingly disparate companions as the bison, elk, bear, dragonfly, moth, cocoon, and spider have for the Oglala a perfectly "logical" connection. The connecting concept underlying these apparently ill-assorted associates is the wind, or Whirlwind. In Lakota mythology, the Whirlwind (*Umi* or *Yum*) is the little brother of the four winds, all five the sons of Tate, the Wind. Whirlwind was born prematurely and never grew up, but remained a playful child, sometimes naughty, but much loved, especially by the beautiful Wohpe, who married his brother the South Wind and who is associated with White Buffalo Woman, bringer of the sacred pipe to the Lakota.

An Unlikely Chain of Associations

It will be appropriate to begin to examine this strange chain of associations with the cocoon; for it is from the cocoon that there emerges, in a manner undoubtedly as mysterious to the non-Indian as to the Indian, the fluttering butterfly or moth. The moth is thus conceived as similar to the Whirlwind due to the "logical" fact that the moth may be no more contained than may the wind. Further evidence of identity of this form with the "formless" wind are the fluttering, wind-producing actions of the wings, a trait possessed by other winged forms, such as the dragonfly, which therefore must also have access to Whirlwind power. The cocoon-encapsulated Whirlwind power is of obvious value to a warrior; having such power, the man would be as difficult to hit as the butterfly or the dragonfly. Also the Whirlwind's playful, twisting movements have power to produce confusion of the mind—according to Oglala patterns of thought, the minds of the enemy.

Another member to be added to this strange assembly of cocoon, moth, butterfly, and dragonfly is the bison, and even tangentially the bear, said by the Oglala to possess power to confuse the enemy. The buffalo is the chief of all the animals, and represents the earth, the totality of all that is. It is the feminine, creating earth principle which gives rise to all living forms. The bear represents knowledge and use of underground earth forces (roots and herbs) in a "terrifying" and strongly masculine manner. It has no fear of either man or animal, and Black Elk, who was both a medicine man (*pejuta wicasa*) and a holy man (*wicasa wakan*) explained that many of his powers to cure were received from the bear.

It has been observed that in winter when a bison cow drops a calf, she is able to blow out from her nose and mouth a red filmy substance which envelops and protects the calf, just as the cocoon protects the developing moth. The imagination of the Oglala has also been stimulated by the trait of the bison bull, who "paws the earth, every now and then deftly scooping up the dust with his hoof and driving it straight up into the air . . . the buffalo is praying to the power of the Whirlwind to give him power over his enemies."[4]

Also included in this apparently unlikely assemblage, through their association with the wind-power, are the spider and the elk. The spider is frequently carried by the wind on fine filaments of web, and is also seen to be a friend of the Thunder-Beings who, in their turn, control the direction of the four winds. Meanwhile, the elk's power to attract females through his bugling call is also seen to demonstrate control over the wind, and Oglala men attempt to simulate this sound on their "love-flutes".

A more detailed account and explanation of these affinities can be found in Chapter IV.

The Sacred Mystery

In all these interrelationships it is evident that the historical-cultural tradition plays an important role in determining the forms selected, their use, and the nature of the values attached to them. These values are expressed with an extraordinary aptness; the correspondences between levels of reality are as if one were the reflection of the other; they flow into each other in a manner that expresses a total, integrated environment.

Intercepting the horizontal dimension to the world of

appearances, there is always, for the Oglala mind, the vertical dimension of the sacred, and in his sacredness there is the sense of "mystery." In sacramentalizing his world of experience, and in recognizing levels of abstraction within and transcendent to this world, the Oglala give place to all components within what for them must be an eminently coherent worldview.

The Oglala

In this book our focus is the Oglala Sioux of the North American Plains. They are a nomadic hunting people. We will especially reflect on their values as they relate to the animals and birds that inhabit their world. The Oglala Sioux, a western division of the Teton Dakotas, is a classic example of a nomadic hunting people. Much of what is included in this book I obtained when I was very young from older Sioux who still remembered the days of the bison and the Battle of Little Big Horn.

Native American Spirituality

So much past interpretation of Native American spirituality has regrettably been forced into preconceived molds of Western, especially Christian, theological perspective. Certain Sioux writings have also contributed to misunderstandings due to the fact that they were extensively edited by non-Indians. The result has often been an over simplification of very complex and subtle realities.

The Oglala's own conceptions of animals within their own value and belief structure is central to this book. I will look at the following questions. What precisely for the Oglala is their idea of "power" as manifested through the animals? And what is the relationship between such forms of power and their experience of a Supreme Being? Who is their *"Guardian Spirit,"* and what is the relationship between such a *"Spirit Power"* and the *"Master of All the Animals"*? What concept of *"Animal Soul"* do the Oglala have? What differences, if any, are recognized by the Indian between animals appearing in *Everyday Experience,* animals in *Dreams,* or animals in *Vision States*? Is the natural–supernatural dichotomy real or is it an artificial reality projected on Indians by "outsiders"? Do Indian peoples have an alternative experience? These questions cut across a wide range of Oglala beliefs and values and lead us to the core of what may be called their religion.

Three Concerns of the Book

I will consider first what animals mean to the Oglala as a cultural resource. Second, I will seek to demonstrate what animals mean in the awareness and values of the Oglala. Third, I will look at what animals mean in the fabric of the daily life of the Oglala.

An Overview of the Book

I will begin by describing those animals within the environment of the Oglala that were essential to their physical and ritual needs. I will then reflect on their physical and behavioral traits and the meanings the Oglala associated with these traits. Here I will especially consider how the Oglala saw certain animal skills and qualities as applicable to the human personality and what spiritual message they each carried. I will then go on to consider the specific techniques by which the Oglala reaffirmed, intensified, and even manipulated the "powers" underlying the animal world. Especially important here are *the vision quest, the medicine bundle,* and personal animal *fetishes.* I will also seek to discover the Oglala experience of animals in their *shamanistic rites,* such as *animal dances* with their songs about animals and animal cries. I will also reflect on the variety of animal representations in their art and crafts. The use of animal names as personal names is especially significant for native peoples. I will look at this particularly in a ritualistic sense. Finally, I will explore what animals mean for the Oglala in terms of their ranking of the "powers." Of special importance here will be an understanding of the *Guardian Spirit* and of their central most important reality, *Wakan-Tanka.*

Chapter I
Bison and Game in the World of the Oglala

When I was ten years of age I looked at the land and rivers, the sky above and the animals around me, and could not fail to realize that they were made by some great Power. I was so anxious to understand this Power that I questioned the trees and the bushes.[1]   —The Author

The essential purpose of this book is to see the environment and animals among which the native peoples lived, through their eyes. We are concerned with Indian values and their experience of their own environment or habitat. Nevertheless it is important to see this same world through the eyes of those "outsiders" who perceive the environment primarily as a series of natural resources, to be selected out and used according to a different set of values. Though what follows is a description of some of the aspects of the environment or habitat of the Oglala, it is impossible to be comprehensive. Such a description would fill an encyclopedia.

The examples that follow were central to the daily life of the Indian. Their daily life reflected a profound understanding of their habitat as a physical reality, as a natural resource. Irving Hallowell put it well, stating: "Their knowledge of the habits of animals would excite the envy of any naturalist. . . . The Indian is no fool . . . the daily round of life, the first hand knowledge of celestial, meteorological, physiographic and biotic phenomena cannot be dismissed as an unimportant factor in the total situation."[2]

The Plains Grasslands

The nomadic range of the western Teton Sioux had the Black Hills (*Pa Sapa*) as its approximate geographic center after 1765. Their range of movements, though, extended out from this center through the central Dakotas to south-eastern Montana, western Nebraska, and eastern Wyoming north of the Platte River. This extensive territory constituted the western "short-grass" and central "mixed-grass" plains, as distinct from the less arid eastern "long-grass" or "true Prairies." The *entire* area of the western Plains and eastern Prairie, however, extended from Saskatchewan and Manitoba in the north, to Texas in the south, from the Rocky Mountains in the west, and as far as Indiana to the east. This vast and complex area of grassland covered more of North America than did any other, approximately one-fifth of the land's surface.

Since these plains grasslands have been described in detail in the past, it is only necessary here to emphasize the importance of the rich grasses and flowering plants of this area. These formed the base and source of a great food chain which originated in these rich grasses and nourished the animals, which in turn provided a food source for other carnivorous beings. The dead gave to the living, and the chain continued with dynamic force. Yet, with inherent fragility, this cycle was to be broken within a short period of about thirty years.

The Indian population's diet, other than the animals provided by the plains and utilized in season, included numerous herbal plants. Wild vegetables and tubers, including wild artichokes, potatoes, prairie turnips (*Timpsila*), Cheyenne turnips, and wild onions, were used in season. The wild fruits they used (which mostly grew in the creek and river bottoms) were Juneberries, gooseberries, wild strawberries, cherries, plums, and arrowleaf berries. Even the redfruit of the cactus, which grows in the more arid regions of the Plains, was an important food source. From the wild rose apples of the Plains, the women made thick soup called *wojape*. In the spring, the box alder provided a source of sugar. Even some kinds of fungi and acorns, which required a complicated method of preparation, have been mentioned as a food source.

The valleys of the Black Hills provided the Oglala with protection in winter and were also an important source of the lodge-pole pine. These trees could be cut already dried on the stalk, providing straight, light poles for the tepees.

The Destruction of the Bison

The bison is the chief of all animals, and represents the earth, the totality of all that is. It is the feminine, creating earth principle which gives rise to all living forms.
—Black Elk

In spite of the seasonal availability of these resources, the greatest nourishing force of the Plains was in the grasses. This prairie supported the vast herds of bison, exploited by the Indians as a major source of food and for a multitude of items essential to their way of life. According to the estimates of Ernest Thompson Seton, the total Plains and prairie area inhabited by the bison was approximately 3 million square miles. Bison living on the Plains numbered approximately 40 million. Those of the prairie area numbered about 30 million, and a total of 5 million were present in other areas. This totaled approximately 75 million head. Based on the most conservative possible estimates, however, Seton states that the number could not have been less than 50 to 60 million. By 1889, excluding small pockets of bison in Canada which numbered not more than 600 head, bison remaining within the United States numbered approximately 256. Considering estimates in early 1840, that the Indians made use of not more than approximately 2 million head annually, and not withstanding the fact of the very real occasional destructive force of blizzards, history presents us here with a dramatic record of man's capability to disrupt a vast and complex ecosystem.

The Bison as an Aspect of the Sacred

A person such as a Black Elk was thus able to describe the act of hunting as being—not representing—life's quest for

*ultimate truth. Hunting is a quest, he insisted, which
requires preparatory prayer and sacrificial purification: the
diligently followed tracks are signs or intimations of the
goal; and final contact or identity with the quarry is the
realization of Truth, the ultimate goal of life.*[3]

The near-total uses of the bison by the Oglala and all the
Plains peoples are indicated in Appendix B. This information is
arranged in categories according to sustenance, tools, and artifacts used in the daily life of the people, and parts of the
animal used in ritual context.

It should be emphasized that because of the overall value of
the bison in Oglala religious beliefs, the animal and all parts
of it express for the people some aspect of the sacred regardless
of what the context of its use might be.

With the exception of the fur, horns, hooves, teeth, sinew,
and pizzle, absolutely all parts of the bison were universally
used as a food resource. Certain parts of the animal were more
prized than others, such as the various innards: liver, pancreas,
heart, and kidneys. The fatty flesh from the hump of the
animal was especially prized by the old people with poor teeth
for its tenderness and nutritional value. Also favored was the
layer of meat near the hide on the back and a still thicker
piece along the belly. Bison tongues also were considered most
delicate by the Sioux. When times were difficult, even the
bison's hide could be scraped, and the chips boiled and eaten.
In very difficult situations, rawhide containers could be cooked.
Bones were cracked, and the grease and marrow boiled out.
Sausages were made from the intestines and filled with pieces
of the best meat, tallow from around the kidneys, and blood.
These sausages were usually first boiled, then grilled over
coals.

Large quantities of the best meat were cut into thin slices
then dried on special racks. This meat, known as *papa*, could
be kept indefinitely. It could also be pounded up, mixed with
tallow and pounded wild cherries, and made into pemmican
(*wasna*) which was kept in rawhide sacks. Pemmican was considered a great delicacy, and an offering of it was especially
appreciated by the spirits.

Considering how efficiently the Indians used the total animal

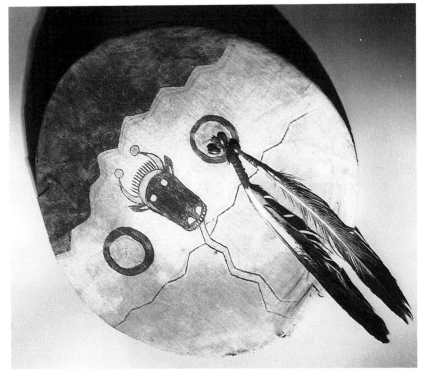

A buffalo shield.

in their diet and daily needs, it is understandable that they were so repulsed by the wasteful non-Indian hide hunters who often took no more than the tongue and hide.

Other Animals of the Plains

When a Plains Indian woman decorates a robe with porcupine quills, she is not just involved in making a useful object aesthetically pleasing, but as a member of a women's quillwork "guild," she is obliged to fast and pray before commencing her work, and she must retain a contemplative attitude as she works with the brightly dyed quills. Because of the formal and initiatory nature of the quillworker's guild to which she belongs, the woman will probably be aware of the identity made by the people between the porcupine and the sun, and that the sun is a manifestation of the Creative Principle. The quills, therefore, which she is laying on in

geometrical patterns established by tradition are really rays
of the sun and thus eminently sacred. The quillworker
has, as it were, trapped the sun, understood as a spiritual
principle, upon a garment now of both utilitarian and spiri-
tual value. These are values which are real and operative
both to the maker and for the wearer of the garment. Neither
art nor what we call religion are here divorced from each
other or from life.[4]

Although the bison obviously outranked all other mammals in terms of the extent of their uses by the Oglala, at all times people would benefit from any available sources of meat. Such secondary resources were essential in times of need when the bison herds could not be located in certain seasons. In such times, the Oglala would often withdraw into the Black Hills where they could have access to woodland and mountain animals, notably the deer and elk, and many smaller mammals (see Appendix D).

After the bison, deer were undoubtedly the most in demand by the Oglala. Deer provided excellent quality hides and meat, a welcome change from the bison's. Soft-tanned buckskin was ideal in weight and quality for men's shirts and leggings, whereas the finer doeskin was of better weight for women's dresses. Soft tanned deerskin was used for many types of sacs, pouches, ceremonial paraphernalia, light moccasins, and as coverings for shields. The owner painted his shield with his protective animal-owner emblems. Deerskin aprons or skirts were worn by Oglala men in the Sun Dance. Rawhide of the black-tailed deer was used for drumheads, and members of the Miwatani Society had deer hoof rattles. The hooves also yielded necklaces, armlets, and other decorations.

As with the bison, all parts of the deer were used, often in ingenious ways. For example, a baby who had no mother was nursed by filling a deer's bladder with warm soup and cutting a small hole in the bottom. The deer's sinew, taken from along its backbone, provided the best-weight thread for sewing its own hide. This soft hide was especially suitable for embroidery work with colored porcupine quills, an art in which the Oglala women excelled.

Many practical and ceremonial uses were made of the

animals and birds which were hunted, trapped, or snared by the Oglala.

More highly prized for fineness than the skins of the doe were the hides of the wild or mountain sheep. From these skins, the women occasionally fashioned dresses or special ceremonial shirts for the men of the Hanskaska Society. These shirts were made of two uncut hides, one for the front and one for the back, which were simply fastened in the appropriate places. It is significant that for all their robes and clothing, the Oglala preferred to cut the hides as little as possible, as if they wished to retain the integrity, and thus the power, of the whole living animal.

Due to the very rapid disappearance of the wild sheep from the Plains after 1870, it is of interest to note George Grinnell's statement concerning these animals:

> In early days wild sheep were very numerous, and very unsuspicious and gentle. Of all the larger food animals they are said to have been the easiest to kill—less shy, even, than the buffalo. Moreover, they were exceedingly abundant in many places, as, for example, on the prairie, near the bad lands of all the streams running through the northern plains country, and about the high buttes that rise from the prairie. In the bluffs along the Yellowstone, White River, the branches of the Cheyenne River, and along the Little Missouri, as well as in the Black Hills as recently as 1860–1870, sheep were very plentiful and were usually killed with arrows.[5]

Entire skins of the fox were worn by men of the Kit Fox Society. Similarly, wolf skins were worn by members of the Wolf Society, or of the Wolf Cult to which they belonged by virtue of having dreamed of the animal. Such "wolf-hide bearers" appropriately acted as scouts for war parties, wearing the hides along their backs and passing their heads through a slit made near the neck.

Otters were sought for their fine fur, which was used primarily for ceremonial paraphernalia. For example, lances carried by the members of the Kit-Fox Society were wrapped with this fur. Bands of other fur, including rabbit fur, were worn around the wrists and ankles of men in the Sun Dance. I have seen medicine sacs made from the whole skin of the otter and have observed that for special occasions, even in contemporary times, the older men will wrap strips of the fur around their braids.

Ermine or weasel skins and elk teeth were used as power-ornaments on dresses. Indeed, virtually any part of the animals might be affixed with aesthetic ingenuity on to eagle-feathered bonnets, shirts, or women's dresses. The people's close association with the animals stimulated their imagination toward utilizing the endless forms found in nature, especially for ceremonial and ritual objects. "Ribbons" of bear gut, for example, were said to have been used to attach eagle tail feathers at the lower end of the Oglala sacred bow. Bear gut has an iridescent surface, and so was considered colorful and beautiful. On the stems of sacred pipes, the whole neck-skin of the mallard duck was placed near the mouth piece, along with dyed horse hair, bison fur, shell discs, or woodpecker feathers.

Feathers of many kinds were worn for their decorative properties or power content, and were also used for fletching arrows. Among those favored were the feathers of the prairie hen, owl, chicken hawk, buzzard, and particularly the eagle. Whistles used in the Sun Dance were made from the wing bone of the golden eagle and had eagle plumes attached to them. Due to its elevated position in Oglala religious belief, nothing worn or used ritually could equal the sacred power associated with the feathers of the eagle.

Hunting Skills and Herd Migrations

In terms of interconnections, a dominant theme of all Native American cultures is that of relationship, or a series of relationships that are always reaching further and further and further out; relationships within the immediate family reaching out to the extended family, to the band, outward again to the clan, to the tribal group; and relationships do not stop there but extend out to embrace and relate to the environment: to the land, to the animals, to the plants, and to the clouds, the elements, the heavens, the stars; and ultimately those relationships that people express and live, extend to embrace the entire universe.[6]

To obtain a continuing supply of these living resources, the

"Buffalo chase under wolf-skin masks" by George Catlin.

Oglala required highly organized techniques of exploitation. Movements of the groupings of the people were in response to movements of the animals or herds. The animals, in turn, moved in accord with climatic changes. The seasonal movements of the bison, which the Oglala believed were controlled by the alternating forces of the North and South winds, resulted in their occasional "disappearance," a natural phenomenon which supported the Indians' belief in an underground origin for these animals.

The close-knit Oglala family groups (or *tiyoapa*) were in reality (for most of the year) extremely efficient hunting units. Leaders of these hunting groups, whether headmen or the four respected "pipe owners" (or *Wakincuzas*), were chosen probably more for their status and reputations as wise and generous providers than from demonstrated success in warfare, although achievement in both areas normally went together. The important civil and police societies (*Akicita*) often had as their explicit function the necessary control of the communal hunting grounds.

Often the Indians' appreciation and utilization of nature's living forms have been treated with romantic sentimentalism. This quality never existed for the Indians themselves, for their hunting endeavors were realistic and often a matter of life and death. For example, I was once surprised at the seemingly "cold" and "matter–of–fact" attitude of the kindly sage Black Elk when he said that the best time to kill prairie chickens is when they are gathered together in a circle for their periodic "dances." Then, with one good shot, the entire lot can be killed. From the Indian's point of view, this attitude was simply pragmatic and realistic, for death by starvation was always a real possibility for the people. Attitudes toward the animals and nature in general were never "materialistic" nor purely quantitative. Rather, the reality of the pursuit of game was intensified and supported by cultural tradition, making the quest for game a religious activity to be prepared for and concluded by Ritual. The quarry was then made into an eminently sacred or power-bearing being.

Chapter II
The Role of Animals in Oglala Life

The animal hunted is sacred-power. So to follow his tracks one is on the path of power. To kill then the animal is to obtain power. All this is wakan. —Black Elk

The Oglala's Observations of His Environment

The Oglalas' successful use of the animals in their habitat implied the possession of a rich fund of knowledge. The very survival of a hunting people and the perpetuation of their culture depended on such knowledge. Interrelated with this knowledge, however, was the individual's inner world of belief and values, which gave cohesion and direction to the society.

Interwoven in both knowledge and subjective interpretation was the culturally conditioned orientation toward the environment. It was imperative that this be taught and transmitted to subsequent generations. The following statement by Lone Man, a medicine man to the Lakota, is instructive:

"I have not much to tell you except to help understand this earth on which you live. If a man is to succeed in the hunt or the warpath, he must not be governed by his inclination, but by understanding the ways of animals and of his natural surroundings, gained through close observation". . . . and after my talk with him I observed them closely. I watched the changes of the weather, the habits of the animals, and all the things by which I might be guided in the future, and I stored this knowledge in my mind.[1]

Writing of the Sioux in 1821, Father De Smet remarked on the keenness of their observations of nature:

> They acquire this practical knowledge by long and close attention to the growth of plants and trees, and to the sun and stars . . . parents teach their children to remark such things, and these in their turn sometimes add new discoveries to those of their fathers.[2]

The Santee Dakota, Charles Eastman (*Ohiyesa*), mentions that every morning when he left his tepee his father would remind him to:

> "look closely to everything you see," and on return he would question the boy for several hours concerning his observations. It was his custom to let me name all the new birds that I had seen during the day. I would name them according to the color or the shape or the bill or their song or the appearance and locality of the nest—in fact everything about the bird that impressed me as characteristic.[3]

For all Souian groups, innumerable examples could be presented by studying the minute details of the natural environment. Brave Buffalo of Standing Rock Reservation is of special interest due to his emphasis on selecting a specific animal for detailed observation. He inferred that the creatures want to communicate with humans, and his questions indicate a concern for more than just phenomenal appearances:

> Let a man decide upon his favorite animal and make a study of it . . . let him learn to understand its sounds and motions. The animals want to communicate with man, but Wakan-Tanka does not intend they shall do so directly—man must do the greater part in securing an understanding. . . . When I was ten years of age I looked at the land and the rivers, the sky above and the animals around me, and could not fail to realize that they were made by some great Power. I was so anxious to understand this Power that I questioned the trees and the bushes.[4]

In this chapter, it will be convenient and appropriate to arrange the many animals involved into three of the four general categories that are recognized by the Oglala themselves:

1. The "four-legged peoples"
2. The "crawling peoples"
3. The birds of the air, including the insects (which are referred to as "the Winged," or the "Nation of the Winged-Peoples")

The fourth category, that of the "two-leggeds," refers to human beings. The close association conceived to exist between humans and birds finds affirmation in Oglala awareness because both birds and man are two-legged.

My Oglala informants invariably referred to all the above animal categories as representing "peoples as we are." A dichotomy, representing additional categories of another order, cuts across the four mentioned above, establishing their relationships to man. This is expressed through a legend which, for the Oglala, establishes legitimacy for the "two-legged peoples." It should be emphasized that the listing of animals discussed below does not include all the living forms of the Oglala's plains and mountain habitat, because a complete and systematic study of these people has never been done. This does not, however, imply that they did not have a rich lore which undoubtedly encompassed all the animals of their environment.

The Bison: Chief of All the Animals

The Bison is the chief of all the animals and represents the earth, the totality of all that is.   —Black Elk

The bison (*tatanka*) constituted, for the Oglala, the major source of practically all their subsistence needs. Exploitation of this resource required patterns of living which placed the Indian continually close to the ever-moving herds. It is understandable that the Oglala should know, in great detail, all the characteristics and habits of this animal.

Such observations were a prime medium through which core values of their culture could find multiple expressions, especially in terms of religious belief and accompanying ritual expressions. As Black Elk explained, the piece of bison hide that is placed on the stem of the Oglala's sacred pipe is "for

A wounded buffalo.

the earth, from which we came." Indeed, on many occasions, Black Elk, who received visions of the bison, referred to this "chief" of all the animals as representing the Earth, the totality of all that is. The great care this animal shows for its young is symbolic for the Oglala. As already described, in winter, a cow which has dropped a calf will spray the helpless animal with a red filmy substance that spews from her nose. This substance envelops the calf so that its body heat is retained. This apparently biological phenomenon was reproduced by the medicine man in the Oglala rites "Preparing for Womanhood."

Also noted by the Oglala, and supported by the observations of naturalists, is the dominant, matriarchal role of the cow in her relationships with blood-related (clan) subgroups within the herd. The old cows, not the bulls, act as leaders. When herds are widely scattered as a result of being hunted, the members of her family grouping always eventually work their way back to her. It also has been noted by the Indians that the unusually fine, silky, much sought-after bison "beaver-robes" came from calves who had become orphaned. These calves were immediately adopted by a number of cows who demonstrated their care by continually licking their coats.

The virtue of hospitality was undoubtedly seen by the Oglala to be a general function of the generosity of the earth, which gave forth the seemingly inexhaustible supply of bison. Many particular expressions of this hospitable generosity actually could be observed. One such affirmation was in the Indian's observation that certain birds (especially the cowbird of the starling family) nested in the wooly fur between the horns of the bison.

The Oglala saw in the bison cow a model for the culturally affirmed womanly virtues, while, in the bison bull, a masculine pole to the earthly qualities was discerned. The Indians observed, for example, that whenever a calf was separated from the herd and was attacked by wolves, the bulls gathered in a circle around the unfortunate animal, protecting it with their formidable horns against the predators. In a similar manner, when the cows slept at night, they were encircled by the protecting bulls. It is undoubtedly in imitation of this trait that the men of the Oglala Buffalo society (*wotawe*) were given to sitting in a circle, wearing their headdresses and robes of the bison bull.

Those familiar with the habits of the bison bull know that before entering into a fight he will violently paw the earth, with appropriate bellowing, and throw clouds of dust high into the air. Associating this action with his own particular needs for warfare, the Oglala conceived that the bull was praying "to the power of the Whirlwind" before going into a fight. By a kind of magical process involving associations and analogy, the Indian conceived that the power represented by this act worked to confuse the minds of the enemy.

The observed dust-throwing trait furthermore stimulated in the Indian's mind a chain of associations linking such seemingly dissimilar natural phenomena as the cocoon, the moth, the spider, the Whirlwind, the Thunder-Beings, and even the elk. It was also observed that the dust-throwing trait was engaged in by the bison not only prior to fighting, but also as a preliminary to mating. Following this display, the Indian observed that the cow then followed the bull away from the herd. Again through analogy, similar sexual power over females was especially sought by the Oglala male.

Wearing a buffalo mask.

"Mandan buffalo dance" by George Catlin.

The Power of the Elk

Recorded information on the Oglala's observations and accompanying views of the elk indicate special appreciation for the physical attributes and general qualities of the bull animal in particular. Among those qualities specifically singled out are his strength, speed, and courage. The powerful form of his massive antlers, and the skill with which he is able to travel with such horns through even the thickest cover, were discerned and appreciated.

In defining certain ideal traits for a man, the Teton Lakota, Shooter, states that the good man should have

> . . . the strength and ability to accomplish his aims. He is brave to defend himself and others and is free to do much good. He is kind to all, especially to the poor and needy. The tribe looks to him as a defender, and he is expected to shield the women.[5]

The Indian also observed that among all the large animals, it

An elk or wapiti.

is the elk who mysteriously has only two teeth, and these he has noted "remain after everything else has crumbled to dust. These teeth will last longer than the life of a man, and for that reason the elk tooth has become the emblem of long life."[6]

Above all, however, the Indian was impressed by certain "mysterious" qualities of the animal's behavior. Examples of this are his custom of traveling alone, and his ability to bugle or "whistle" in such a manner that the elk cows are irresistibly drawn to him. These are the specific traits that demonstrate the presence of strong "sexual power," underlying most of the Oglala elk-lore. This has been found to be a dominant motivating theme for the Elk Society, in quasi-magical cults, and in a wide range of customs.

It is especially appropriate here to stress the Oglala's views and ideas about the elk. It seems that it is not the physical elk— nor the physical form *in itself* of any other power-manifesting animal—that is looked to as the source of power. Rather, as Clark Wissler points out:

The elk is taken as the incarnation of the power over females, the real (ie, physical) elk is regarded only as the recipient of such power. The power itself is conceived of in the nature of an abstraction similar to our conception of force. The fact that the elk seems to act in conformity with the laws governing this power is taken as evidence of its existence. Then the idea of the Indian is that the elk possesses the knowledge necessary to the working of the power. Thus a mythical, or hypothetical elk, becomes the teacher of man.[7]

A similar interpretation of the elk and his power has been advanced by H. H. Blish:

The Elk was closely associated with the Indian idea of love and sensual passion. Supernatural power lay behind manifestations of sex desire: consequently, numerous mythical creatures were thought to control such power, and of these, the bull elk was the most important.[8]

Supporting the concept of the "hypothetical elk," and yet representing an approach from another dimension, is the especially interesting Santee Dakota text of Boas and Deloria. A young Dakota, who denies to his father that anything is sacred (*wakan*), tries to shoot an elk with his arrows, but they turn to down. The rock he then uses against the animal turns to fluff. This *elk who cannot be killed* then talks to the youth saying: "It is not good that man tries to own those walking on earth who live."

The importance of the concept of a hypothetical animal must be emphasized, for such ideas are crucial to an understanding of the Oglala's structure of reality.

The Double Nature of the Deer

It was noted in Chapter I that the skins of the deer were highly prized by the Oglala and used for numerous articles of clothing and necessary equipment. In spite of the large demand for deer hides, it is curious that the literature on the Oglala, and indeed my own notes, have yielded very little information on values and awareness relating to this animal. The ambivalent and wary attitude toward the deer may account for the apparent unwillingness of the Oglala even to talk about the animal.

References have been made to the swiftness of the deer, to the mysterious manner in which the deer could hide himself when hunted, and also to the "magical" power of certain songs which may make the deer appear. It is said that Teal Duck, in a Sun Dance, had a black deer's head painted over his mouth "because the deer could endure thirst for a long time without losing its strength."[9] It has also been pointed out by the Oglala, Left Heron, that the deer's flesh is good to eat because:

> Early in the morning and late in the morning the deer picks out good things to eat. He goes among the young trees and eats the cherries and the young leaves. He tastes all that is good. So the deer-flesh will strengthen you well.[10]

The presiding attitude toward the deer, however, is one of ambivalence. To the Oglala, deer manifest dangerous power and have a double nature, which forked–horned animals generally represent. The white-tail deer has been reported as "an animal helper who gives man its form to help him on his quest." But a negative and dangerous power seems to be especially associated, in Oglala legends, with the black-tail or wood deer. The black-tail has been known to appear to young men as a beautiful maiden, luring them to a lonely spot away from camp; but when the man approaches her, she turns into her true self, which is a doe. Death is usually thought to result from such an encounter, even if—or perhaps, especially if—the man, in anger, should subsequently kill the animal. Should the man not die, however, he would always be thought to possess great power. Black Road, the originator of the Oglala Bow Society, apparently secured his personal power from this source.

The Oglala's belief in the mysterious and dangerous qualities of the deer result from his observation of a particular odor in the deer's hoof, which is believed to become fine perfume when the animal turns into a woman. Through this perfume, the doe is aided in luring the young man away to his death.

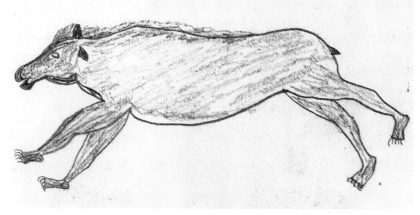

A black bear.

The Fearlessness and Healing Powers of the Bear

The Bear is quick tempered and is fierce in many ways.
Yet he pays attention to herbs which no other animal notices
at all . . . we consider the bear as chief of all the animals
in regard to herb medicine.
　　　　　　　—Two Shields, Standing Rock

The Bear has a soul like ours, and his soul talks to mine
and tells me what to do.　　—Bear with White Paws

If an ambivalent attitude was expressed by the Oglala toward
the deer in what may be called a "feminine" mode, a similar
attitude of ambivalence was held in relation to the bear, but
in a "masculine" mode. A polarity may be discerned in com-
paring views of the bison with those of the bear. The bison
represented the nourishing and life-giving force of the earth
in a manner that expressed the principle of ideal womanly
virtue. The bear represented knowledge and exploitation of
underground earth forces (the roots and herbs), but in a "terrifying" and strongly masculine manner.

The Oglala, like all Indians who had any contact with the
bear, were understandably impressed with the fierce power and
unpredictable qualities this animal represented. The Indians
know of the bear's lack of fear for either man or animal. They

noted the bear's characteristic habit of digging with massive claws into the earth for roots and other underground products of the earth, and wondered at his mysterious habit of sleeping during many of the winter months. As with the other animals, the Oglala men sought to assimilate these powers which were manifested through the bear form.

Black Elk, having received "bear powers" through dreams and in the vision quest, often would be observed emitting low bear-like growls when he was ill or particularly troubled. When asked why he made such bear-like sounds, he explained, "I have the bear's power, and when I am in need of it this gives me strength." Black Elk, who was both a medicine man (*pejuta wicasa*) and a holy man (*wicasa wakan*), explained that he had received many of his powers to cure from the bear. Although I was not able accurately to verify the actual number of medicines known to him, many Oglala said that he knew over two hundred distinct herbs. Along with songs and prayers, these herbs were used in healing ceremonies. (Proper prayer and song were also used during the process of procuring the needed healing herbs.)

Many examples can be found as evidence of the association of curing with bear power. Standing Bear mentioned that the bears spoke to him and gave him bear powers. The bears told him to recognize all things of nature and to observe and learn from them.[11] Two Shields, the Lakota from Standing Rock Reservation, observed the following:

> The bear is quick-tempered and is fierce in many ways, and yet he pays attention to herbs which no other animal notices at all. The bear digs these for his own use. The bear is the only animal which eats roots from the earth and is also especially fond of acorns, Juneberries, and cherries. These three are frequently compounded with other herbs in making medicine and if a person is fond of cherries we say he is like a bear. We consider the bear as chief of all the animals in regard to herb medicine, and therefore it is understood that if a man dreams of a bear he will be expert in the use of herbs for curing illness. The bear is regarded as an animal well acquainted with herbs because no other animal has such good claws for digging roots.[12]

The fact that the bear himself digs up and eats the many roots and herbs of the earth, as Two Shields had indicated, led to the assumption on the part of the Indian that the bear was almost invulnerable; and invulnerability in warfare was a prime quality sought by the Oglala.

Of special interest is Two Shields' further reflection that the effectiveness of the bear's medicine-power was due to his dual nature. "The bear is not afraid of either animals or men and it is considered ill-tempered, and yet it is the only animal which has shown us this kindness."[13] Therefore, the medicines received from the bear are supposed to be especially effective.

The bear's entire nature seems to be composed of contrary, or shifting qualities. These are witnessed in his ill-tempered aggressiveness, as contrasted to his passive dormant state in hibernation. His habit of standing on his hind legs has supported beliefs in the reality of metamorphosis. When confronted by a bear, the Indian cannot be sure if the bear is a man in bear form or vice versa. It is not surprising, therefore, to find that even the bear's soul is thought to be special among the animals.

The Strength and Tenacity of the Badger

The superior claws and digging power, as well as the vicious and tenacious fighting qualities of the badger (taxideataxus), led to the Oglala's association of this animal with curing practices and desired powers for warfare. In both these skills, the badger seems to have been closely associated with the bear; however, because of the badger's relatively small size, the powers for curing associated with him seem to be directed, appropriately, to medicines for children. Eagle Shield, who stated that he had received powers from the badger in a dream, claimed to have power for curing children, although he also indicated that: "some consider his medicine [the badger] stronger than that of the bear, as he digs deeper and further into the ground."[14]

As the underground Power of the earth, inherent in the roots and herbs, came to be represented through the form of the bear, so too the badger seems to be associated with a parallel concept. In an Oglala legend, for example, the hero Iron Hawk is told that the badger is "an earth animal—he lives and digs in the earth. This food means that you also must live on the earth. It is good for you . . . this is holy earth and you are going to walk on the earth."[15]

The essential and justifying power-principle underlying the Oglala *Akicita* Badger Society (*Ihoka*) lies in the observed and sought-after strength and fighting qualities of the badger. The term *Ihoka* itself "seems to mean badger mouth and was explained as referring to the characteristic grimaces and growlings of the badger when attacked."[16] It should also be noted that the "no-flight" or "no-retreat" custom observed in warfare by certain members within the Societies certainly had its model in the fighting behavior of the badger.

The Earth Powers of the Skunk

In the mind of the Oglala, even the skunk was important; he seemed to be associated with mysterious earth powers in a manner similar to the badger. Although the skunk possessed a well-known power unique to himself which no doubt was recognized, he was also observed to manifest the courageous and tenacious "no-flight" quality possessed by the badger. It was apparently for the sake of possessing just this power that Dakota chiefs, as observed by Schoolcraft, "had the skins of skunks tied to their heels to symbolize that they never ran, as that animal is noted for its slow and self-possessed movement."[17]

Bears, badgers, and skunks seem to be conceived by the Oglala as expressing a certain positive–negative polarity of powers inherent in the forces of the earth. Gophers, on the other hand, seem to be linked to predominantly negative associations. It was believed that "scrofulous sores on the neck under the jaw are said to be caused by gophers. These animals can shoot at persons in a magical way with the tip of a species of grass, wounding them very mysteriously."[18] Negative evaluation of the gopher is also indicated by the Blackfoot, for whom the animal represents the states of distraction and casualness, both traits generally disliked by Plains Indians.

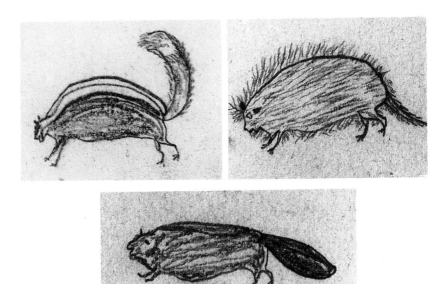

A skunk, a porcupine and a beaver.

The Speed, Wisdom and Solidarity of the Wolf Pack

Few animals have claimed the attention of the Plains Indian warrior more than has the grey wolf. Because he was observed to be a fast runner of great endurance, the scouts of Oglala war parties wore wolf hides and were said to be "very fleet of foot like the wolf." Because wolves have always been wanderers, they know everything. Brave Buffalo has said that he prayed to the wolves when he wanted to locate game, and they always told him where to secure it. Always, the wolf gives advice. Therefore, scouts return to camp howling like wolves. Wolf songs taught in dreams or visions, as well as the actual howl of the wolf, are thought to have special power. An example of this is a Dakota legend of a wolf who teaches a man a song, and when he howls, wind is created. At another howl, fog appears. The wind served to confuse the enemy, and the fog lent invisibility to a war party. The old uncle of Ohiyesa gave the following advice, based on observation of the wolf's habits:

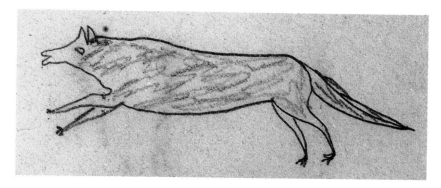

A coyote.

You ought to follow the example of *shunk–tokecha*. Even when
he is surprised and runs for his life, he will pause to take one
more look at you before he enters his final retreat. So you must
take a second look at everything you see.[19]

This same person observed that:

The grey wolf will attack fiercely when very hungry. . . . But
their courage depends upon their numbers; in this they are like
white men. One wolf or two will never attack a man. They will
stampede a herd of buffaloes in order to get at the calves; they
will rush upon a herd of antelopes for they are helpless; but
they are always careful about attacking man.[20]

This example of strength through solidarity of the pack was
certainly taken as a model for the solidarity and cooperation
characteristic of members of Oglala Societies, and particularly
those of the Wolf Society (*Han Skaska*). Members of this Oglala
War Society seem to have associated curing power with the
wolf. It is said that they could cure the sick and remove arrows,
although they were never to cure wounds.

The Brule Sioux, Charging Thunder, recounted a dream of
an old wolf who taught him to make a pipe:

telling me to smoke it when I was on the warpath and saying
that the smell of the pipe would be so strong that the enemy
would not detect my approach and thus I would be able to steal
their horses. The old wolf said that by the aid of this pipe I
would be able to outwit the wisest and craftiest of my enemies.[21]

Of special interest in this account are the words in the song which the wolf taught Charging Thunder in a dream, "a wise spirit, I met." This reference to "spirit," rather than to the wolf as such, again shows that for the Oglala, as for the Plains Indians in general, each animal was really a crystallized projection of the abstract spirit.

The Persistence and Gentleness of the Fox

The fox was considered to be persistent, yet was gentler and less aggressive than the wolf. This is undoubtedly the reason the Wolf Society was predominantly a War Society, while the Kit-fox Society (*Tokala*) was one of the *aki cita* or Policing Societies whose duties centered less on warfare and more on camp life and hunting activities. According to Standing Bear:

> the fox had knowledge of underground things hidden from human eyes, and this he shared with the dreamer, telling him of roots and herbs that were healing and curing; then he shared his powers of swiftness and cleverness as well as gentleness.[22]

In this gentleness, there was strength and courage, as indicated by one of the songs of the Fox Society: "I am a Fox. I am supposed to die. If there is anything difficult, if there is anything dangerous, that is mine to do."[23]

The Importance of Even the Smallest Creatures

It should be noted here that for the Oglala, no animal is insignificant. Black Elk related that "one should pay attention to even the smallest crawling creature for these too may have a valuable lesson to teach us, and even the smallest ant may wish to communicate to a man."[24]

Two examples of this qualitative rather than quantitative attitude toward living forms were evidenced in his explanation. The little "buffalo bug," for instance, was known to tell scouts the direction in which buffalo could be found, for they are especially sensitive to the vibrations of the earth. Also, they always faced in the direction of a herd, which could be a great distance away. Secondly, Black Elk mentioned the tiny woodgrub, "to whom we should all be especially thankful" for he is used in boring out the "breath-passage" of the wooden pipe stems.

The Oglala observed the rabbit and sought its qualities of agility and what appeared to them to be "humility." Black Elk mentioned that "the men also put rabbit skins on their arms and legs, for the rabbit represents humility, because he is quiet and soft and not self-asserting—a quality which we must all possess when we go to the center of the world."[11,25]

Paul Beckwith, too, has noted that rings of white rabbit skin were actually not worn, but tied into the flesh of the shoulders and legs of men in the Sun Dance. Due to the frequent association in many cultures of the rabbit, or hare, with the moon, it is of interest to note Louis Meeker's statement that "the initiated know that the eye of the rabbit is the moon, and that the figure we see on the face of the full moon is the reflection of the rabbit in his own eye."[26]

Hides from the mountain goat were prized by the Oglala. These hides were difficult to secure and, when well-tanned, were particularly soft and pliable, and thus desired by women for dresses. In spite of the infrequent contact with this animal, J. O. Dorsey has noted a society of those who dreamed or had visions of the goat. These people obviously were impressed with the characteristic abilities of this animal:

> Goats are very mysterious, as they walk on cliffs and other high places; and those who dream of goats or have revelations from them imitate their actions. Such men can find their way up and down cliffs, the rocks get soft under their feet, enabling them to maintain a foothold, but they close up behind them, leaving no trace.[27]

The Creatures That Live in the Water

The turtle is a wise woman, she hears many things and says nothing.   —from the Buffalo Ceremony

Conceptions of the Oglala relating to the turtle seem to depend on observation. The Indian found the shells, with their strongly etched designs, as well as the turtle's amphibious nature and

A turtle.

its ability to adapt so completely to an aquatic environment while remaining essentially a "four-legged" land animal remarkable. This association with earth and water suggested to the Oglala a feminine power for the animal. In the context of the purifying rites for preparing a girl for womanhood (the Buffalo Ceremony), the Oglala conductors of the ceremony offered the young girl advice by saying that, "The turtle is a wise woman. She hears many things and says nothing." Characteristically, the conductor then described further turtle-like qualities that apparently a warrior would desire. "Her skin is a shield. An arrow cannot wound her." J. R. Walker indicates a further association with womanly powers:

> The symbolic basis for the representation of the turtle . . . is found in the belief that the turtle has power over the functional diseases peculiar to woman, and also over conception, birth, and the period of infancy. The eating of the living heart of the turtle is regarded as a positive cure for menstrual disorders and barrenness.[28]

Association of the turtle not only with the feminine physiological characteristics of women, but indeed with the totality of the earth, is indicated by Meeker, presumably writing of the Oglala:

> Only the initiated know that the turtle is the earth, and that

we inhabit the shell on his back.[11,29] . . . These associations
linking the turtle with the earth, the waters, and feminine
powers in general help to clarify the frequent use of the turtle
amulet. This amulet contained the navel cord of the newborn
child, for it is this cord which nourishes, or connects man to the
feminine earth-source of sustaining power. It has been explained
further that since the turtle, like the lizard, is difficult to kill,
"it was fitting that their protective power should be enlisted as
guardian of the individual's substance. . . . The vigilant protection of one's entity was essential to the Sioux sense of well-
being.[30]

Snakes are considered by the Oglala to have power, some
being more powerful than others "because if they bite they
would kill." It was also considered "unlucky" to dream of
snakes, for they "are said to be terrible; they seek to enter a
man's ears, nose, or mouth and should one succeed, it is a
sure sign of death. No good comes from snakes." This negative
evaluation of snakes also finds expression in the Oglala myth
of the Sacred Buffalo Cow Woman who brought the sacred
pipe to the people. The young man who had lustful intentions
toward her was seen to be consumed by "terrible snakes," so
that only his bones were left.

It is significant, however, that in the Oglala ideas of animate
beings, it is not possible to find examples of a form for which
there is an exclusively negative evaluation. Thus, it was the
snake who was the originating power in the founding of the
Sacred Bow Society. The dualism involved in such shifting
attitudes provides a significant example of the meanings
inherent in the important Lakota adjective *wakan*, which has
so often been interpreted with the exclusively positive impli-
cation of "sacred power." Actually, there are multiple nuances
for the term, as was clearly indicated by the Oglala, Sword:
"Anything may be *wakan* if a *wakan* spirit goes into it. Thus a
crazy man is *wakan* because the bad spirit has gone into him."[31]

The Supremacy of the Winged-Peoples

*The most important of all the creatures are the wingeds,
for they are nearest to the heavens, and are not bound to*

Two wild geese.

the earth as are the four-legged, or little crawling people.
Their religion is the same as ours. They see everything that
happens on the earth, and they never miss their prey.
                                                —Black Elk

Attachment to the qualities manifested in the birds (Winged-Peoples) is so strongly integrated into Oglala culture (and Plains Indian cultures in general) that Black Elk was given to declare that "their religion is the same as ours." According to Black Elk, "the most important of all the creatures are the wingeds, for they are nearest to the heavens, and are not bound to the earth as are the four-legged, or little crawling people."[32]

Other observations leading to this special position of the birds concern their ability "to see everything that happens on the earth," and "they never miss their prey. Then like the eagle you will overcome all enemies. He never misses that at which he strikes."

The eagle, hawk, swallow, dragon-fly, all possess great speed in flight and ability to strike swiftly and surely; and they seem to bear a sort of charmed life before bullets, arrows, hail and lightning, for one does not find them killed or injured by these forces.[33]

Birds had a special association with the circle, a form which always had special connotations of power for the Plains Indian.

> Our tepees were round like the nests of birds, and these were always set in a circle . . . a nest of many nests, where the Great Spirit meant for us to hatch our children.[34]

Regarding the ceremony of securing the sacred tree for the Oglala Sun Dance, Deloria has said that before the tree is cut, gratitude is expressed to it for allowing all the birds to raise their young in its branches.

Just as the bison was considered to be chief over all the animals of the earth, so, among the birds, the greatest power was ascribed to the eagle. In the minds of the Oglala, certain symbolical possibilities are assigned to the beings of the air in distinction to those of the earth. It may be said that the eagle holds priority over all non-human living beings, because the eagle "flies higher than all other birds," "sees everything," and "moves through the skies in the sacred form of the circle."

Black Elk attributed his association with this bird to the Supreme Spirit, *Wakan-Tanka*. The unusual power connected with the eagle is clearly indicated through the elaborate ritual that accompanied the catching of live eagles. Men carefully wrapped the bird in sage "to avoid being injured by the eagle's power." His feathers could not be plucked until after a four-day period, for only then could his excessive power be safely handled. Also, in pulling the feathers, the men were supposed to cry to show respect for the Eagle's spirit, so that more eagles might be taken at other times.

The special powers and qualities associated with the eagle clarify the great importance given to all parts of this bird. Of particular value were the plumes, feathers, and the wing bone (femur) from which whistles were made to use in the Sun Dances. "The whistle itself symbolized the great Thunder-power, and its note was the cry of the eagle which was a representative of the Thunder."[35] A further extension of meaning was stated by John Blunt-horn: "If you are attacked, take a whistle of eagle bone, blow upon it. This will confuse the enemy and make them easy to overcome."[36]

Feathers and plumes of the eagle have been used universally by the Oglala and Plains Indians for a wide range of purposes, with a multitude of associated meanings. Feathers have been either cut or painted, and worn as a "feather language" to express war honors or special honors obtained in the hunt. Feathers and plumes have been thought to lend special powers to the wearer. They were also associated with the very life breath of the living being.

Essentially, both eagle plumes and feathers represented particular expressions of the essential values and meanings conceived to be inherent in the bird itself. Black Elk explained that the worn feather is a reminder of, or, more specifically, is for him the real Presence of the Great Spirit.

Indications are that the eagle can be associated with the sun, and its feathers are considered to be the sun's rays. Eagle feathers on a sacred shield with their painted protective devices are thus said to be solar rays. This association, in part, explains the Oglala custom of periodically moving such shields and their tripods, so that they may always face the sun.

The traits of the wolf were seen to represent, for the Oglala, attributes and qualities desired in warfare. The avian counterpart is the crow or raven. These birds can best be described within the context of one of the *akicita* Societies, the *kangi yha*, or Crow Owners. One of the members of this Society, the Lakota Eagle Shield (*wanbli-waha cunka*), states that: "We want our arrows to fly as swift and straight as the crow. The crow is always the first to arrive at the gathering of the animals in the Black Hills."[38]

Also, the crow "can find dead things no matter where they are hidden." This all-observing ability of the crow has been seen to be associated with the particular powers of certain Yuwipi practitioners. The raven's characteristics parallel those of the crow. His "watchfulness" has led camp sentinels to wear as a "distinguishing mark . . . a collection of two or three raven skins fixed to the girdle behind the back in such a way that the tail sticks out horizontally from the body. On the head too is a raven skin split into two parts and tied so as to let the beak project from the forehead."[38]

It is the owl who outranks all other birds because of his power of sight in the darkness.

The owl moves at night when men are asleep. The medicine-

man gets his power through dreams at night and believes that
his dream is clear, like the owl's sight. . . . So he promises that
he will never harm an owl. If he did so, his power would leave
him. For this reason some medicine-men wear owl feathers. The
medicine-man also regards the owl as having very soft, gentle
ways, and when he begins to treat the sick persons he is supposed to treat them very gently.[39]

Little Warrior (*Ozuye Jigala*), who died in 1952, was one of the
best known of the contemporary Oglala *yuwipi* men. Among
other animal spirits, his power was received from the owl. It
is said that he was always able, in the darkness in which his
ceremonies took place, to find lost objects through his owl
"spirit helper." I was always impressed with the gentle owl-
like ways of this dignified man who was widely sought after
for his curing powers.

   Due to the nocturnal habits of the owl, however, there seem
to have been ambivalent attitudes toward the bird, and he was
also associated with death. In Oglala mythology, for example,
ghosts appear after an owl is heard hooting in camp. I recall
a time when a man insisted on leaving his car when he noted
the presence of a bunch of owl feathers. Whether the associations with the owl, or with any animal, are positive or
negative, the form is still the bearer of power and this may be
utilized for the purposes of the people. Thus, the owl-powers
are important to the Oglala Owl Society (*miwatani*). This bird
was believed to be responsible for the origin of the Society,
since the people say that: "The owl and the buffalo appeared
to the originator in a dream and told him about the organization and the regalia."

   In contrast to the owl's association with obscure night-
power, the meadowlark is connected with the clarity and good
things of the day. Undoubtedly, this is due to its beautiful
song, which is always heard in the early mornings on the
prairie. The Oglala say:

   The lark is a cheerful woman. She brings pleasant weather, she
   does not scold. She is always happy . . . if you are cheerful like
   the lark, then you will be chosen by a brave man, and you will
   have plenty and never be ashamed.[40]

The voice of the lark evidently so impressed the people that

Black Elk told me these birds actually speak Lakota and can be understood. Left-Heron also stated this: "Many a word the lark utters an Indian can understand." During the Oglala Buffalo Ceremony, in which the powers of many animals are invoked for the protection and purification of young girls, Walker recorded a shaman's song: "The meadow lark my cousin. A voice is in the air," and explained that "by claiming relationship to the lark the shaman claimed power to influence for fidelity." By saying, "a voice is in the air," he implied that the influence for fidelity pervaded the camp.

The Oglala observed that upon the approach of a storm, the woodpecker (yellow-winged) gives a particularly shrill call similar to that made by the eagle wing-bone whistle. This bird, therefore, has also become associated with the Thunder-Powers. Accordingly, its feathers have been observed to be attached to Sun Dance whistles and "are supposed to put the individual also in a position to speak to the Thunder."

The swift-flying swallows have also been noted to precede the coming of a thunderstorm. In a dream experience received by Lone Man, a Lakota from Standing Rock, the "riders in the cloud" gave him a swallow charm (*wotahe*):

> If I were in great danger and escaped alive I attributed it to the charm and sang a song in its honor. The song relates to the swallow whose flying precedes a thunderstorm. When I sang the song of my charm, I fastened the skin of a swallow on my head. This bird is so closely related to the thunderbird that the thunderbird is honored by its use. The action of a swallow is very agile. The greatest aid to a warrior is a good horse, and what a warrior desires most for his horse is that it may be as swift as the swallow in dodging the enemy or in direct flight. For this reason my song is in honor of the swallow as well as of my charm.[41]

The Wind-power of the Insects

To the non-Indian, insects are obviously not similar to birds. Nevertheless, the Oglala see all creatures who fly (ie, those who manifest possession of the powers of the air) as being grouped together. The elusive and swift-flying capabilities that certain members of this group have in common, along with their accompanying invulnerability, were qualities sought by the Indian. At least two members of this group, the dragonfly and the moth, or butterfly, especially attracted the attention of the Oglala.

Siya'ka, a Lakota from Standing Rock, gives general indication of the value of these flying beings, recounting a dream experience received during a retreat:

> All the birds and insects which I have seen in my dream were things on which I know I should keep my mind and learn their ways. When the season returns, the birds and insects return with the same colorings as the previous year. They are not all on the earth, but are *above* it. My mind must be the same.[42]

On a more utilitarian level, Clark Wissler states for the Oglala: "The dragonfly is venerated as a being possessed of the power to escape a blow. They say it cannot be hit by man or animal, neither can the thunder injure it."[43] Hence, the dragonfly is also in touch with a power the Indians covet. The Oglala associated the fluttering, wind-making qualities of the moth's wings with the underlying powers of the Whirlwind. They noted that moths and butterflies proceed mysteriously from the confinement of the cocoon; so, this form itself took on special significance and, thus, appeared stylistically represented on a number of objects. The actual cocoon was often taken with a portion of the twig or surface upon which it was found, then wrapped in an eagle plume or down, and worn on the head. This was regarded as a perpetual prayer to the power of the Whirlwind. The sacred cocoon bundle apparently was conceived as being charged with potentiality.

As with so many power-forms, the Indians attached dual functions to the cocoon–Whirlwind concept. The power became applicable to what the Indian desired for himself. Through the proper manipulating prayer, the power-quality could be so projected as to work to the disdvantage of the enemy.

> In the whirlwind somehow and somewhere resides the power to produce confusion of the mind . . . it became the prayer of the Indian that the minds of his enemies should be confused. The buffalo bull is said to pray to the power of the whirlwind before going into a fight.[44]

The Unique Powers of the Spider

> Iktomi *(the spider) was a man in the early days, just like any person. He was the first who attained maturity in this world. He is more cunning than human beings. He names all people and animals, and he was the first to use human speech.*   —Black Elk

Typical of the complex and ambivalent attitudes of the Oglala toward the spider (*Iktomi*), is my dilemma in assigning the spider to one of the four Oglala categories of beings (ie, the "two-legged peoples," the "four-legged peoples," the "crawling and swimming peoples," or the "Winged-Beings"). The special conceptions held by the Oglala for the spider are undoubtedly due to the fact that of all creatures it is Spider who "walks" on legs (although it is on four pairs rather than on two). It is Spider who is also so close to the ground that he may be thought to crawl and, although he may not swim, some spider-like beings do demonstrate control over the water's power since they walk on its surface. Finally, although spiders do not "fly," they nevertheless appear to have control over the air due to the use of their often invisible threads. In fact, the spider, in the Oglala's observations and legends, occupies such a very special place that a special section is here given to him outside of the established categories.

It was Spider who first attained maturity in this world. He is more cunning than human beings. He names all people and animals, and he was the first to use human speech. Even toward the supernatural monsters, Spider demonstrates this arrogance, establishing himself as the Creator himself: "I made this earth and the sky and the sun and the moon and everything. You are one of the things I made. You were a little grey thing and I threw you away."[45]

In typical fashion, Spider beats this monster by using a clever trick. In his assumed role of Creator, Spider becomes a type of Culture Hero, for the Oglala believe that arrowheads and stone war clubs were made by him and had only to be found lying in piles at certain places on the earth. Because of the great powers of Spider, it is believed that the people should not kill him directly, but do him in by resorting to a spider-like trick.

It is difficult to establish whether the positive traits of Spider outweigh the negative ones. Spider's actions obviously suggest a trickster, a liar, a deceitful and arrogant being. "Spider fools everything on earth, in the water, and above the earth in the air." All the unpleasant things in the world come about through Spider, which is the reason he is associated with those other mythological monster-beings – *waziya*, *Iya*, and *Untehi* – who bring mischief into the world. It is *Ikotomi* who often hides the faces of the Sun and the Moon. Death itself was made by *Iktomi*, as a necessary condition to existence, so that room may be made for other beings in the world. It is *Iktomi*, usually, who sets out his nets in which to catch living beings.

The actual physical characteristics and traits of the spider which form the basis for most of the rich lore are evident. The Oglala have observed the Creator-like capability of the spider to fashion a web out of his own body, his ability to rise into the air on his often invisible thread, and the fact that insects are caught in his web. The sting of some spiders is poisonous. That mastery of all these traits exists in a being so small obviously impressed the Oglala.

Through these beliefs, the importance given to the spider's web as a "magical-motif" in a wide range of associations and representations is clarified. For instance, the spider's web was thought to possess power to protect from bullets.

> The observed fact that a spider manufactures a web, and that this web is not destroyed by bullets or arrows (since they pass through it, leaving only a hole), is cited by some individuals as the basis for the conception that the spider has power to protect people from harm. On the other hand, the spider is spoken as a friend of the thunder; and it is a general belief that the thunder will never harm the spider-web, or, what amounts to the same, that the spider-web itself is a protection against thunder.[46]

Members of the Sacred Bow Society have rawhide images of the spider hanging from their eagle-bone whistles, suggesting again "an association of the spider with the thunder," (ie, with the higher powers, powers that can protect and strengthen). In the Oglala's stylized representation of the spider's web, the four corners of this web-design stretch out toward the four directions. These directions are conceived as the home of the four winds, and of the four Thunder-powers. Emphasis on this association of the spider with the Thunders is noted in this web-design, and the lightning forms depicted around the design. As a technique for applying these powers to the specific protection of children, the Oglala would make a hammock resembling the spider web, strung between four trees. The child was then placed on it. "This is to bring good fortune to the child." To carry these associations even further, note that painted on the Oglala "courting robe" is the stylized chrysalis-like representation of the Whirlwind. This is considered to be the younger brother of the four winds. It is thus associated with the "bundle" in which the spider wraps its eggs, a container of Whirlwind-like power-potentiality.

> The protection or aid of the whirlwind was secured by prayers and these were symbolized by the cocoon worn upon the person, by its image in stuffed buckskin, or by its graphic representation, sketched or painted. The power of the whirlwind was supposed to have been associated with the power of the spider-web.[47]

Here again, the moth was seen to have access to wind-powers which he could recreate through the force of his wings.

There are specific associations of the spider-powers with womanly qualities. The Oglala say that: "The spider is an industrious woman. She builds a tipi for her children. She gives them plenty of food. If you are industrious like the spider . . . then you will be chosen by a brave man, and you will have plenty and never be ashamed."

It is also believed that the spider was "regarded as a power influencing women because of his cunning." Similar power over women, already noted in connection with the elk, adds another element to a linking chain of associations, and explains the presence of the spider *and* elk painted on the Oglala "Courting Robe." This robe was apparently manipulated so that the sought-after girl would step on it. The "catching-power" of the spider and his web could then be strengthened "by the owner carrying a dead spider in his mouth."

A Sioux buffalo skin.

Conclusion

Of a social and ethical order, affirmation is seen to be given to the virtues of hospitality, good disposition, generosity, fidelity, industriousness, and honesty. Religious or spiritual attitudes and values are expressed in terms of "loftiness" of mind, and attention and attachment to the "supernatural" powers. These were manifested in the sacred and mysterious sanctions underlying all natural phenomena. Affirmed was the life-giving force of the Earth, expressed in the bison, while spiritual values were reflected in the high-flying and all-seeing Eagle, or in the "loftiness of mind" implied generally in all birds.

Individual or social behavior or attitudes which ran contrary to norms were held up and emphasized through the negatively presented traits of certain beings such as the spider. Finally, the Oglala love of freedom was expressed and affirmed through the moth-containing cocoon in which, ultimately, the wind as life-activing power, could be contained.

Although the terms "utilitarian," "ethical," "moral," "religious" or "spiritual" have been used, these represent non-Indian types of categories which tend to distort the reality of the Oglala's experience. The Oglala obviously view the forms of their outer world through the selective structuring which they have received from their cultural traditions. But their reflective minds and keen observations have led them to seek out forms which reflect their values. These values can be called completely "logical" within the total framework of their worldview. The Oglala's use of the environment reflected a dual process in which the external natural environment actively influenced them in a manner best described as both positive and creative.

Chapter III
Animal Guardians and the Vision Quest

—— ⌐ ——

It is through the vision quest, participated in with physical sacrifice and the utmost humility, that the individual opens himself in the most direct manner to contact with the spiritual essences underlying the forms of the manifested world. It is in the states achieved at this level that meditation may be surpassed by contemplation. Black Elk has thus said that the greatest power above all in the retreat is contact with silence. ". . . for is not silence the very voice of the Great Spirit."[1]

The Vision and the Dream Experience

In this chapter, the Indian's rapport with the animals and birds will be seen within a number of institutionalized patterns of belief and behavior. Through participation in these patterns, it will be noted that the relationships with the animals are shifted onto the participatory and conceptual planes. They are also reformulated through this participation, for the individual's encounter with the animal brings about a qualitative growth in intensity. Then, through religious and social mechanisms, the powers that accrue from such intensifications are catalyzed and integrated into the fabric of the culture.

The central core of what has been called "modes of intensification" can be seen to be the vision quest, or the vision itself. Secondarily comes the dream experience, with both of these

An elk-head whistle.

phenomena acting as a source for a host of institutionalized forms and behavior.

The man or woman who has a vision or dream experience of an animal or bird (for these animate forms constitute the essential medium of the experience) is normally required to "capsulate" the experience in a "fetish." Often a complex of fetishes was contained within a "medicine bundle." A medicine bundle also contained the subsequently acquired animal's skin or a significant part of its body. Usually, the experience is further "concretized" through the formal enactment of a more or less public dance-drama ceremonial. This ceremonial contains the accompanying songs and other requirements "taught" to the individual by the vision being. In this manner, the experience is not only actualized, but is sustained for him or her through time. It also provides a means by which the people may participate themselves in the represented power.

This procedure offered a means for the socialization of what, to the individual, was a superhuman experience. It also ensured its integration within the total network of relationships. The power-containing bundles could have been central to larger ritual complexes. This may have been especially true where such bundles were designated as being for the welfare of the total group. Personal names also may have been associated with, or directly derived from, the encounter with the spirit-animal in a vision. Additionally, this animal's form was painted on clothing, shields, or tepees.

The majority of the several types of Oglala Societies originated from an individual's encounter with the vision animal. This animal gave specific instructions for the organization's function, code of behavior, and required paraphernalia.

Hanbelachia, *or "Crying for a Vision" . . .*

> *Often the sacred experience comes in the mysterious appear-*
> *ance of an animal or a winged being, or perhaps in one of*
> *the powers of nature. A special message is often communi-*
> *cated to the seeker, and this will serve as a guide and*
> *reminder throughout the person's life. After three or four*
> *days one returns to camp where a sweat lodge has again*
> *been prepared; within this lodge the candidate will explain*
> *the vision or dream which will be interpreted by the guiding*
> *elder, who will then give instructions as to what should*
> *now be accomplished in order to insure the continuity of*
> *the participation of the spiritual throughout the person's*
> *life. From such experiences have come the "medicine bund-*
> *les" with rich and complex rites specific to each bundle and*
> *their ceremonial opening on special occasions. They have*
> *also been the origin of sacred types of art forms, such as*
> *the painted shields, or special songs of power, or even the*
> *great ritual dances. . . . What is remarkable about the rites*
> *of the vision quest among the Plains peoples is that it is*
> *accomplished not just by special people . . . but that every*
> *man or woman after the age of puberty is expected to*
> *participate either once or even continually throughout his*
> *or her life.*[2]

The vision quest was basic to Plains Indian cultures and a critical factor to individual role and status. It was a necessary antecedent sanction for all important undertakings and has been richly documented in literature. Among the Oglala (for whom this quest was termed "crying for a vision," (*hanbelachia* or *hanblecheyapi*), at least two general features are germane.

First, although the quality of the dream, vision, and degree of frequency varied considerably (especially between the medicine man and others), the quest was participated in by virtually all the men. Women also participated, though less frequently and with less rigorously formal elements. Second, although the vision experience could involve seeing or hearing any form or force, in an overwhelming majority of cases the vision encounter was with a wide range of animal and bird beings. One or more of these could become the individual's "guardian spirit(s)."

Since great importance was given to the encounter with animal forms in dreams, as well as in the vision, it is important to determine what distinctions were made between these two phenomena. In Lakota, a certain distinction is made between *hab le'*, referring to the vision through fasting, and *wi' hab la*, the dream. Ruth Benedict clearly states that *vision* was not a synonym for *dream*. The precise nature of the distinction in the mind of the Oglala, however, is not easily defined. Black Elk, a shaman of considerable note, recounted to me that a man seeking a vision may sleep, for "it is very often during sleep that the most powerful visions come to us; they are not merely dreams, for they are much more real and powerful."

This reference to a vision in the sleeping state seems contradictory. Yet, in the Indian's experience, both dream and vision are intimately related, and indeed seem to merge into each other. The dream, for instance, may predispose the individual for receiving a vision. In turn, the vision may condition the individual for the reception of certain qualities of dreams. This kind of reinforcing process seems to be indicated by Densmore:

> To a white man, the term "dream" is connected with unconsciousness, but the Indian term implies an acute awareness of something mysterious. Dreams and their songs may come to an Indian in natural sleep if his mind is conditioned to such an experience, but the first important dream comes to a young man in a fasting vigil.[3]

For the Oglala, it seems that distinguishing between dream and vision is of little or no concern for the recipient often recorded encounters with animal beings which took place in the dream state and which held the same power as if the experience had been a waking vision. Among the Standing Rock Lakota, for example, Charging Bear dreamed of thunderbirds, the wolf, and the buffalo. Brave Buffalo dreamed of the buffalo, elk, and wolves; and Siya'ka dreamed of the crow and the owl. There was no question here of the loose use of the term "dream," for the accounts were prefaced by such remarks as "I fell asleep and dreamed." Subsequent to these dreams, protective power, knowledge of medicines, sacred songs, or other demonstrable powers were acquired by the individual. These powers were no different from those obtained through the vision. I recall Black Elk's evident emotion and intensity as he recounted what he described as a dream:

> I was taken away from this world into a vast tipi, which seemed to be as large as the World itself, and painted on the inside were every kind of "four-legged being", "winged-being," and all the "crawling peoples." The peoples that were there in that lodge, they talked to me, just as I am talking to you.[4]

There is ample evidence to demonstrate the fact and frequency of the waking visionary experience, in accord with non-Indian definitions. These and many similar accounts seem to demonstrate that for the Indian these two kinds of experiences are essentially equivalent. In both these phenomena, there is evidence of conditioning processes which contribute to the intensification of the interrelationships with animal forms. These experiences go beyond and are deeper than those encounters which originally were described for the ordinary observations of the waking experience. There is a shift to another level of understanding, which is so conditioned by the religious tradition that a superhuman dimension breaks through these animate forms of everyday experience. On this level, the Oglala is no longer encountering the phenomenal animal, but rather an archetypal "essence" appearing in the forms of various animal beings.

The nature of the encounter with the living forms of nature, or with the spirit that appears in such forms, could be experienced according to the persistence, receptivity, or capabilities of the individual who was seeking. The nature of the encounter could not be controlled. The experience presented responses of the powers to either implicitly or explicitly stated concerns. Such needs ranged from the purely utilitarian to the highly altruistic or purely spiritual—which need not be mutually exclusive. Whatever the motivation, the endeavor and response were always interwoven with intensely religious sanction and conditioning. The quest and resultant vision did not always involve formal acquisition of a guardian spirit. Normally, however, the successful encounter was with a bird or animal, or rather with a power in the guise of a specific animal, and it was through the help of this power that the desired goal or quality could be achieved.

The elements of either the dream or vision experience could take on a number of forms or combinations of forms. However, throughout these expressions, a similar pattern is evident in which the following sets seem to appear with regularity:

1. Association of the animal or bird spirit-form with the powers of the four directions (which appear in conjunction with the aspects of these powers, the Thunder-Beings); the apparition frequently involving four beings, or sets or multiples of four.
2. The appearance of the vision form being heralded by audible messages, often in the form of questions or instructions to the lamenter.
3. The seeker commonly being transported either to another terrestrial location, such as a beaver's lodge, or away from this world.

This last set occurred frequently in the visions of Black Elk. The Oglala Black Horse also experienced this: "Now you are between the sky and the earth. Your Grandfathers living between the earth and sky will help you in medicine to save life on earth."[5]

Metamorphosis is a frequent occurrence. Men may turn into animals and vice versa. One species of animal might shift into another, or an animal may take on a plant form when that plant is to become a sacred medicinal herb. Frequently, it is an animal who finally appears and becomes the seeker's guardian spirit. It is also often noted that the sacred area (from which the seeker does not move during his quest) is miraculously spared rain or hail. Finally, the dream or vision songs, taught by the animals to the seeker, appear with very set traditional musical patterns. Even the messages expressed within the song form share sets of common themes.

It is obviously impossible to describe with any scientific accuracy the real nature of the dream or vision experience. What has been authenticated is, that for the Indian, the experience was real—more real, perhaps, than what is perceived in ordinary waking experiences. Scientific inquiry must define limits, but it cannot judge these types of knowing which cannot be understood in terms of scientific method.

A buffalo drum.

The Fetish as the Physical Symbol of the Vision

Following the vision or dream, and in accord with the interpretations and instructions given to the recipient by his sponsor, the seeker secures the type of bird or animal which appeared to him. The animal is then prepared in a ritual manner by the medicine man. This animal form, or a specific part of it, is either worn or carried in a special bundle. For the bearer, this bundle then becomes a concrete expression of his experience. It is the physical symbol of his vision, and it is the most sacred thing he can ever possess. This ensures continuity to the meaning and intensity of the initial experience.

Some fetishes were exclusively personal. Certain other types, called *wotawe* in Lakota, were buried with the owner upon his demise. Other types of animal-bearing bundles were communal. These were kept through succeeding generations by specified "Keepers." Still others were specific to the smaller groups of certain Societies or Associations.

This section will be directed firstly toward describing typical types of fetishes and bundles, and secondly toward clarification of the attitudes held in relation to these forms. The central purpose here is to deduce types of attitudes and values held by individuals toward such forms. The following selection should provide a meaningful sampling.

The great tribal bundle of the Oglala contains not an animal, but the most revered stone (pipe-stone) Buffalo Calf Pipe. This "came" to the people many generations ago. The association of this ritual implement with the bison, or bison principle, should be noted here. The original legend of this pipe and bundle is well known. The essential feature is the Oglala belief that it was brought by a very beautiful woman who stated that she represented the Buffalo tribe. It also should be noted that she was associated with virtue. In leaving the people, she transformed, in four stages, into a white buffalo cow. This account is perfectly comprehensible within Oglala belief, since the bison is associated with the generous producing or "giving" Earth-principle, and also with ideal womanly virtue. Further, the red stone of the pipe bowl is conceived to be identified with the earth, even to the blood of the earth. To these linking associations may be added the Oglala belief that the White Buffalo Cow Lady was really *Whope*, wife of the South Wind. *Whope* represents all the beautiful growing things of the earth, so long as the South Wind has power over the North Wind. It is impossible not to consider the phenomenon of the North–South migrational movements of bison, which further binds together this series of interrelated associations. For the Oglala, this constitutes a coherent and integrated totality.

The great importance of this Buffalo Calf pipe, and its bundle

containing other sacred objects, can be noted in the legend of
the Buffalo Cow Lady:

> By this pipe the tribe shall live. . . . The Tribe as a whole shall
> depend on it for their necessary needs. You realize that all your
> necessities of life come from the earth below, the sky above,
> and the four winds . . . it will take you to the end . . . for as
> long as the pipe is used, their people will live; but as soon as
> it has been forgotten, the people will be without a center and
> they will perish.[6]

The intensity of belief and attitude toward the Buffalo Calf
pipe is illustrated in the account told to me by an Oglala of
the time. An Agent at Pine Ridge, who was antagonistic to
the people's religion, took away the pipe bundle and locked it
up in his office. The subsequent bellowing of a bison calf,
which continued day and night in the Agent's office, resulted
in the rapid return of the sacred object to the people. On
another occasion, it was told that two men, who had once
seen the pipe during one of the very rare ritual bundle-
openings, made drawings of it and took these to Rapid City
to sell. On their way across the prairie, however, both men
were struck by lightning and killed. It is curious to note that
the photographs and drawings made by Sidney Thomas of the
bundle, pipe, and other ritual contents, do not at all corre-
spond to descriptions given to me by at least four Oglala. In
1948, I visited the "Keeper of the Pipe," Eli Bad Warrior, but
very properly was not even allowed to see the bundle. Did
Thomas see some other pipe bundle?

Central to these beliefs of the coming of the pipe is the fact
that the Buffalo Cow Lady calls the people "my relatives,
brothers and sisters" and says, "we have met as belonging to
one family. . . . I am proud to become a member of your
family—a sister to you all. The sun is your grandfather, and
he is the same as me."[7]

Established in "legendary time" is the custom of the men,
when they had finished smoking the pipe together in a ritual
manner, to say *"mi taku oyasin"* ("we are all related"). Here is
affirmed the pervading conception of an essential and mysterious (*wakan*) bond, binding together the people, the animals,
the earth, and all that is. The use of reference to generational

levels in this affirmation of relationship lends emphasis to recognition of distinction within unity based on conceptual levels. This pattern has been repeated frequently by the Oglala.

Of the individually owned bundles, several types should be described. Those belonging to the *pejuta-wicasa*, or medicine men, are used specifically for purposes of curing. Always the underlying sanctions for both the ritual procedures and the specific components of the bundle are derived from dream or vision experiences. In her excellent account of several medicine bundles used by the Standing Rock Lakota, Densmore identified many types of herbs, along with a number of animal skins and parts of animals that were used for cures. Also significant were the sacks themselves, made of mink or badger paws. The sack contained bear claws, the foot of an eagle, eagle claws, matted deer hair, and the bone of the elk.

Certain medical practitioners were known as *Yuwipi* men. This indicated that they not only had the power to work cures, but also had access to spirits who could convey information concerning lost objects. They also had access to spirits who could provide information about subtle psychological and spiritual problems of the patients.

One such *Yuwipi* man was Little Warrier (*Ozuye Jigala*), an Oglala of Kyle, South Dakota, who was a close friend of mine until his death in 1952. This person was probably the most important of all Oglala medicine men in recent times. He had hundreds of remedies at his command, all of which had been revealed to him by the animal or bird spirit-beings contacted during frequent spiritual retreats. Following one of these quests, I was told that the spirit animal helpers had revealed information about a cure for tuberculosis. Since these matters are normally kept in great secrecy, it was not desirable to try to ascertain which of the animal helpers were involved, or what were the remedies that had been revealed. I did know, however, that the Chief of Little Warrior's helpers was the owl.

In his account of Fools Crow, another Oglala *Yuwipi* practitioner, Wesley Hurt states that "Fools Crow's guardian is the red-headed woodpecker, a skull of which he ties to his pipe stem during the rite."[8]

In this work, Hurt indicated three classes of medicine men:

the *wapiye,* who use only herbs; the *Yuwipi,* who cure, foretell
the future, find lost objects, and give demonstrations of magical power; and the *Ghost Doctors,* who use herbs, make less
use of magic, and have the pipe ceremonial as a central component of their rites.

A crucial dimension to all these rites of curing is found in
the Oglala's recurring affirmation that it is not the individual
practitioner who works the cure, nor is it the actual herb or
bear claw. Rather, these are simply the phenomenal channeling
intermediaries through which the intangible spirit-power oper-
ates. Black Elk, whose own knowledge and skills cannot be
defined, made it clear to me that "the power does not come
from me, but from the Power above which is the source of all
powers." Old Buffalo similarly expressed it when he described
the recovery of his sick niece: "It was *Wakan-Tanka* who saved
her life. . . . She lived in answer to my prayer."

The often confusing manner in which the term "medicine"
has been used in the literature on the Plains Indians undoubtedly has its basis in precisely these attitudes. The Indians seem
both to identify superhuman powers with some substantial
support and to recognize an essential distinction. This apparent
confusion is certainly related to possibilities of multiple levels
of understanding by the *wacasa-wakan* (sacred-power men) as
compared to the understanding of the majority of the people.

Certain modes by which these experiences are crystalized
and channeled give continuity to the experience in accord with
conditioning cultural patterns. It may now be asked, to what
extent, or with what precision, may the qualitative nature of
the acquired animal guardian be defined? This spirit-power is
actualized in the experience of the Lakota himself. The guardian was received in the personal quest and not through other
possible "secondary" means.

It has been noted that, first, all men were expected to seek
a "tutelary spirit" through a vision. Not all men received such
favor, but those who did experienced great variations in the
quality of the experience received. For some, experiences were
of such an intense and recurring nature that the recipient might
become a medicine man. Encounters with certain types of
vision phenomena may obligate the recipient to fulfill certain
types of specified roles in his life. Those who dreamed or had

visions of the Thunder-Beings or of dogs were destined to become *hehoka*, or contraries. Those who dreamed repeatedly of the bison, or of Double-Woman or the Deer-Woman, might be destined to be *berdaches*, although they may or may not be medicine men.

There is an intimate correlation between the appearing form and the resultant quality of power, knowledge or skill acquired. Densmore has summarized this point well in her discussion of spirit-animals:

> A bird flying high was believed to help a warrior. A bear, which has good claws for digging herbs, was supposed to aid a man gathering herbs with which to treat the sick. Each animal appearing in a dream gave its own power to the dreamer.[9]

The problem still remains of defining just what the nature of this power is, and of determining if it is this power which essentially becomes the individual's guardian spirit.

Clues to the nature, for the Oglala, of this power or of the nature of the acquired guardian spirit, may be gained from a ranking of the animals. Their underlying spirit-power may be inferred from their specific qualities (which have been discussed already). Grizzly Bear, for example, was understood to be Chief of the underground earth forces, conceived in a negative and terrifying way. Bison was Chief, in an exclusively positive sense, over all animals of the surface of the earth. Eagle was seen to have supremacy over all the flying beings. Some animals outranked others in terms of their "attracting" powers, while Spider outranked all in terms of cleverness. Throughout the range of examined Oglala conception, expressions of rank may be implied, but in a sense, it is secondary and fragmentary.

With the exception of the bison, explicit expression is lacking of the animals' "Owners," "Bosses," or "Keepers of the animals." This is particularly evident when compared to such a strong and explicit expression among the Algonkin and other circum-polar peoples. Although frequent references were found to suggest the Oglala had clear ideas of an underlying abstract and qualitative power-principle, rarely do such references indicate the type of authority power-structure as conceived of by the Algonkin. The lack of such an awareness among the Oglala may be a result of the close interrelationship between forms of political organization and patterns of religious belief. Indeed, the "democratic" nature of Oglala society is well known. Even the distinctions made between the medicine man and others of the society did not represent a wide separation. From another point of view, animals and birds, or rather their Spirits, are not conceived by the Oglala in any absolute sense as controllers over the destiny of human beings. The animals are thought of as witnesses to the affairs of humanity, and specific powers could, in humility, be requested.

The question, then, still remains: How are the Oglalas' awareness and views of their guardian animal spirits formulated? On the basis of data gathered, it can be said that the guardian spirits of the Oglala represent qualitatively differentiated manifestations of powers. These awarenesses are obtained by men and occasionally women under certain conditions and are based on the animate forms of the natural environment. Such spirit power-bearing forms are then possessed by individuals. The forms are supported by the fetish or the fetish-containing bundle. This fetish acts as a source to ensure the continuing actualization of the expressed quality in the life and behavior of the individual. This would also reinforce the continuing affirmation of the reality and intensity of the initial vision or dream experience. The quality of this experience as well as the accumulative frequency of recurring experiences, may then determine whether or not this individual is to fulfill specific roles, such as that of the medicine man. The quality of the experience, or even the fact that no vision experience was achieved, may be instrumental in influencing the individual's character and personality. From the Oglala's own point of view, the experience may be the cause or origin of success or failure in a wide range of social, subsistence, or military activities.

The Enactment of the Vision Experience

As complement to the individually oriented "vision quest,"
one could mention the great communal "Sun Dance,"

referred to by different terms across the Plains groups. For this great complex of solemn rites, ceremonies, fasting, sacred song and dance fulfills not just the particular spiritual needs of the actively participating individuals, but also those of the entire tribal group gathered in circular camp for the occasion. The event is indeed for the welfare of the entire world. These are ceremonies, interspersed with special sacred rites, which celebrate world and life renewal at the time of spring.[10]

The first requirement imposed on those who have received visions was to secure the living form of the animal encountered and prepare it in accordance with instructions given by the chosen medicine man. In addition, the recipient was normally obliged to ensure that this found its extension of "socialization" through enactment. This usually took the form of a dance ceremonial involving medicine songs and display of paraphernalia which had been made explicit through instructions received in the vision experience. Enactment was expressed in a variety of manners. Some might be complex and highly formalized dance ceremonies. Often though, the individual simply displayed specific paraphernalia, sang those songs which had been received, or provided a demonstration of powers. Whatever the expression, the psychological and social functions of these observances are clear: by dynamically enacting or dancing out the "passive" experience, a reintensification of the initial experience resulted. The total being participated in, and thus integrated, the superhuman experience. The larger social group was thus able to participate in the experience. This served to condition or orient members of the group, especially the youth, toward this quality of experience. In the process, the continuity of core cultural values was assured.

Many types of Oglala dances, songs, or accompanying ceremonial paraphernalia obviously have been secured through historical contact with other groups. Always where such traits are accepted, it is because they may be adapted to conform to the Oglala's own patterns. In addition, a large number of songs and dance-forms are specific to types of Dream Cults, or to Civil or War Societies. Many of these had their origin and "operational force" in the animal powers received through dream or vision by the original founding member.

The Dance Ceremony

An excellent example of what is probably the most complex type of Dance Ceremonial enactment of a vision is provided by Black Elk's account of his "Horse Dance." The Ceremony was preceded by fasting and the ritual sweat, both for Black Elk and for the two medicine men who were assisting. A tepee was set up in the middle of the camp circle and images representing aspects of the visions were painted on it. These included white geese, to signify the North, together with images of horses, elk, and bison. In this sacred enclosure, an altar was established, and songs received in the vision were taught to the two medicine men.

Sixteen horses were secured. Four of these horses were black, symbolizing the West, four were white, for the North, four were sorrels, for the East, and four were buckskins for the South. A bay horse was provided for Black Elk, similar to the one he had ridden in his vision. The horses were painted with lightning stripes and hail spots. The riders, too, had lightning bolts painted on their limbs and breasts. They wore white plumes on their heads to make them look like geese. A spotted eagle was painted on the back of Black Elk's horse, at the place where he would sit. Black Elk himself was painted red with black lightning. He wore a black mask and a single eagle feather at his forehead.

In the actual dance, the vision songs were sung by the four teams of riders. The horses pranced to the rhythm as they moved to the four directions of space, circumambulating the camp, and finally charging down on the central tepee. Along with the horses, all the people in the camp danced and all sang the sacred songs. So similar was this enactment to the original vision that Black Elk stated that the vision came to him again: "what we then were doing was like a shadow cast upon the earth from yonder vision in the heavens, so bright it was and clear. I know the real was yonder and the darkened dream of it was here.[11]

In this account, it is of interest to note the association of lightning with the horses. This is in accord with the Oglala belief that "the lightning has wings and rides on a horse." Also, "the stallion is said to have power to herd the mares, lead them about, and subject them to his will. His power is supposed to have been given by the Thunder-horse, or the Thunder."[12]

Ceremonial use of the horse has also been noted by Vine Deloria. In the Sun Dance, a man might be accompanied by his horse, who had been tied in the lodge for a full day without taking food or water; the horse was said to be dancing with his owner. Deloria also noted that, on occasion, a man's back would be pierced and the reins of the horse would be tied to the two wounds. The appearance of the horse, both in the vision complex and in the Sun Dance, provides an example of the facility and completeness with which this particular "innovation" became totally integrated into Plains culture. It further demonstrates the force of natural phenomena, as interpreted by historical cultural tradition, and serves as a formative or conditioning agent for the quality of the received vision or dream experience.

The Dream Cult

A number of Oglala ceremonial dances were based on the experiences of a grouping of men or women who shared a common vision of a particular animal. "The animal which appears to a man in a vision during his religious fasting determines to which society he must belong." Two examples of this type of Dream Cult are the Elk Cult and the closely related Black-tail Deer Cult. These two cults were participated in by young men and occasionally by women. In these dances, the participants wore masks with the horns of the elk or deer. Hoops were carried with imitation spider's nets in the center, and attracting mirrors were flashed to "catch the eye of a girl and bring back her heart." Love and sexual desire were interpreted as manifestations of the working of some magic or supernatural power. The participants danced with steps and cries specific to the animal being impersonated. They believed that when they stamped their feet they made magic. The underlying magical principle that was affirmed and made operative can be understood through the descriptions presented in Chapter II. Wissler indicates that at times *all* "the animal cults tended to dance together in one great fête at which time they masqueraded according to their respective cult animals. Some supplementary unpublished data we have makes this clear."[13]

In addition to the Dance Cults of the Elk or Deer dreamers, there was a society of people who had received revelations from the buffalo. Bush-Otter called this the *tatang ihanblapi kin*. "All such men who dream of the buffalo, act like them and dance the buffalo [bull] dance. And the man who acts the buffalo is said to have a real buffalo inside of him."[14]

Through the use of imitative techniques, accompanied by song and strong rhythms, the reality of the dance drama became so intense that the participants obtained a state of realization or trance. For them, there was an inner identity with the bison or with his spirit principle. The dancer's affirmation, that he had "a real buffalo inside him," did not represent simply a metaphorical statement for him. Such "identification" must normally have been the object of many of these types of animal dance-impersonations.

The cult of the Buffalo Dreamers was probably participated in exclusively by medicine men. This would be true especially for the members of the Bear Cult, since not only the ability to cure but also dangerous qualities have been associated with this animal. Women were never members of this cult. They were not supposed to dream of bears, although at least one exception has been noted. As in the dance performances of the other cults, the medicine men of the Bear Cult wore the entire skin of the bear. Wissler recorded:

> They may run about the camp growling and chasing people. They may sit around like bears, and feeling around upon the ground, dig up a turnip and eat it with grunts like the bear. They may even fall upon a dog, tear it to pieces, eat the liver and some of the flesh raw. Also, in battle they may attempt to frighten the enemy by such actions.[15]

Most of the Oglala Civil, War, or Chief Societies were named after their "founding animals." These societies had their own songs and dance-forms through which the qualities of the respective animals were displayed. Among such Societies were the Buffalo Bulls (*Tatanka Wapahun*), Wolf (*Hanskaska*), Crow Owners (*Ka gi yuha*), Kit Fox (*Tokala*), Badger (*Ihoka*), and Owl (*Miwatani*).

Expressions of Power-Traits

Relationships to the external environment were apparently limited only by the range of a people's imaginative receptivity. This receptivity has been seen to be both supplied and screened by the intervening historical and cultural heritage of the people. Visions, dreams, dance-forms, songs, and all the rest express the rich range of possibilities.

Women of a Prairie Chicken Dance Association hopped about and made noises like prairie chickens. In the medicine dance, women imitated the peculiar call of the female swan. In the ceremony prior to cutting the tree for the Sun Dance, men acted like wild animals. They howled like wolves when taking the sacred Sun Dance Tree to camp. During the ceremony, the women uttered the shrill cry of the screech owl. Whistles were made out of the eagle's wing bone, and used by the dancers in the Sun Dance. The whistle itself symbolized the great Thunder-power, and its note the cry of the eagle. Such whistles were also used for other purposes:

> If you are attacked, take a whistle of eagle bone, blow upon it. This will confuse the enemy and make them easy to overcome. Then like the eagle you will overcome all enemies. He never misses that at which he strikes.[16]

In addition to the eagle wing bone whistle, the flageolet (see Appendix B) was associated with the elk and his power to attract women. Some of these "love-flutes" were carved at their lower ends to represent the open beak of the crane. The Big Twisted Flute, conceived to be an especially powerful instrument for love-medicine, has been depicted with the carved head of a horse. Frances Densmore, who undoubtedly knew more about Teton Sioux music than any other scholar, indicated that "music to them, in its highest sense, is connected with power and with communication with the mysterious forces that control all human life."[17]

Among these techniques for communication with power, one

of the most powerful is song. One example, the Dream Song, was very personal and sacred to the possessor. It was believed to have been received directly from the bird or animal encountered in a vision or dream. Within such songs resided the particular power of the tutelary. In many of these songs, the animal or bird states his own name. In singing the song, the singer would tend to conceive not only a contact with the animal's power, but an actual type of identification with the animal.

It should be emphasized that in the Societies that bore the names of animals, the legendary founder was believed to be an animal. Initial contact with this creature was established through a dream or vision. In this encounter, the animal benefactor transferred the "character" or concept of the function for the Society to an individual. This individual subsequently taught the complex to the people. Involved in this complex were detailed instructions for the ceremonial power-paraphernalia, as well as the ceremonial procedures for the use of this equipment. The high ideals set for members of these Societies (thought to have their sanction in the founding animals) were bravery, generosity, chivalry, morality, and fraternity for fellow members. Here again, the animals of the habitat have been singled out. These animals were also conceived as sanctioning sociocultural organizations which were of the greatest importance to the functioning of the total social order.

Possibly the Wolf Society (*Hanskaska*) outranked all the other Societies due to the importance of this animal in Oglala ideas and values. The Society's functions were associated with war. Members must have "big hearts, and never show anger." That they were looked to for leadership is indicated by the fact that among the society's members were the "four grand councilors" of the Oglala: American Horse, Crazy Horse, Man-Afraid of his Horses, and Sword.

The Sacred Power of Personal Names

Thus, to name a being, for example an animal, is actually to conjure up the powers latent in that animal. Added to

this is the fact that when we create words we use our
breath, and for these people and these traditions breath is
associated with the principle of life. . . . It is because of
this special feeling about words that people avoid using
sacred personal names, because they contain the power of
the beings named, and if you use them too much the power
becomes dissipated.[18]

The complex questions of an Oglala's personal name can be
discerned through (1) the outstanding importance of the name
in Oglala values, (2) modes by which personal names are
acquired or given, and (3) the relative importance of the animal
name-type in terms of frequency of use.

Even to this day, I have noted that the Oglala avoid referring
to any individual's personal name, preferring names based on
relationship, in accord with generational levels. This custom
applied not only to interpersonal relationships, but also in
reference to the abstract powers of earth and sky, and to
relationships with all manifested forms or powers of the world.
The name essentially "fixes" for the bearer a kind of relationship with the qualities of that to which the name refers. This
relationship is personal, private, and takes on the character of
the sacred. Densmore mentions that "many tribes of Indians
avoid mentioning a man's name . . . that which remains
unspoken must be considered in the study of any deep phase
of Indian thought."[19] The term "Wakan-Tanka" was not used
in ordinary conversation either. It was considered too sacred
to be spoken except with due reverence and at a proper time.
Personal names, then, bear sets of implications critical within
Oglala ideas. Names imply relationship, protection, favor, and
influence from the source of the named. Names indicate affiliation, connote power, and have sacred import.

Explicit and graphic statements of this power of the personal
name are illustrated in pictographs of Oglala names. The out-
line of the head of the individual is attached by a wavy line
to the animal, bird, or sign hovering above. Mallory correctly
interprets this technique, which is more complex than can be
indicated here.

The waving lines above the head signify the sacred, and are
made in a similar manner as that for prayer or voice. . . . The

word medicine is in the Indian sense . . . and would be more correctly expressed by the word sacred, or mystic, as is also indicated by the waving line issued from the mouth.[20]

The first name of an Oglala child was given shortly after birth. This name may be given by the father, and it might be the name belonging either to the oldest living grandfather or to a deceased and respected grandparent. First names could also be given by an important medicine man who selected the name from his own dream or vision experience. Edward Curtis mentions, for example, that "the name bestowed on an infant was always one suggested by some animal or object seen during one of his [the medicine man's] fasts, and the accompanying prayer was taught him during a vision."[21]

Later in life, the child was given an informal play name, or occasionally a *winkete* name. This name could be given to the child by a transvestite (who not infrequently was a medicine man) and was rarely used when speaking to a person or about a person. When the child grew up, he or she would acquire a formal and serious name, received or validated through some important act or adventure. After a boy returned from his first war party, he was given a name by an uncle or brother-in-law. Later this was exchanged for a name earned by his own great deeds. A man could assume his father's name only after having performed acts of such valor as to entitle him to the honor.

Very commonly, the young man received his formal name through his own dream or vision experience. Typically, there was a correlation between the temperament and orientation of the individual, the quality of his dream, and his acquired name. The warrior might dream of a roving wolf, the hunter of a buffalo. Leaders of Societies could also confer names which were appropriate for members of the respective Society. Wissler recorded that Little Wolf, leader of the Wolf Society, gave the following names to nine members of a war party: Gaunt-Dog, Black Wolf, White-Wolf, High-Wolf, Fast-Dog, No-Dog, One-who-won-the-victory-Dog, Dead-Dog, Red-Dog. Four additional men were also given the names: Big-Wolf, Slow-Dog, Yellow-Wolf, Black-Dog. Wissler also mentions that names could be "thrown away" at a victory dance, and a

Yanktona – *Lone-Dog Winter Count.*

relative might be invited to select a new name. Afraid-of-Bear got this name from Red Cloud after he threw away his old name of "Clam."[22]

Useful sources for the study of Oglala personal names may be found in the Red Cloud Census, the Oglala Roster, Cloud Shield's Winter Count, and American Horse's Winter Count. The Red Cloud Census was made under the direction of the famous chief at Pine Ridge, South Dakota, in approximately 1880. The census included 289 persons, many of whom were heads of families and adherents of Red Cloud. These people did not represent all the Indians at that agency. The so-called Oglala Roster includes the personal names of eighty-four heads of Oglala families in the band of the northern Oglala. Chief Big Road is said to have given the Roster to Agent Major McLaughlin in 1883. Together, these lists contain 373 names, and present sufficient sampling to index the importance of the animals in Oglala personal names. Appendix E presents all those names from both listings that have direct or indirect reference to animals or birds.

In the listings, it is noted that of the principal Oglala Chiefs, four bore animal names, and the fifth, Big Road, depicted his name in pictograph with a bird emblem. Further, of the 178 chiefs listed for the Oglala in 1883, virtually all bore names that had reference to birds or animals. Of the 373 names listed on the two registers, only three names were of composite animals, and those were combinations of mammals with the Eagle: Eagle-Bear, Eagle-Elk, and Dog-Eagle.

Almost two-thirds of the 373 recorded Oglala personal names refer to birds and animals, which strongly supports other data. This affirms the intensity and pervasiveness with which animals and related ideas have become integrated into the fabric of Oglala belief and culture.

White Buffalo Cow Woman: the Originator of Major Rituals

Similar modes of spiritual conceptualization are involved in the making of dwellings and ceremonial structures, whether it be the tipi, the domed sweat lodge, or the sun dance lodge of the Plains. . . . All such dwellings are created in imitation of the process of the creation of the world itself, and all such structures are conceived to be both a model of the universe, and microcosmically of man, who is also a world containing a sacred center.[28]

The Oglala trace the origin of their major rituals to the White Buffalo Cow Woman. She is the one who brought the sacred pipe to the people and who revealed herself to be a bison. As such, she was a representative from the "buffalo people." Actually, only one of the seven central rites of the Oglala plus the rites of the pipe were said to be directly revealed by this legendary Culture Heroine. Nevertheless, she foretold and sanctioned the successive appearance of the remainder of the rites to be received through the individual vision experience. The purpose of what follows is not to describe these rites themselves, but to indicate the manner by which concepts of the bison support the presiding theme of the rite.

"The ceremony of the Spirit-Keeper," the first of the Oglala's seven rites, had its inspiration in the coming of the White

Buffalo Maiden. Everything was done in accordance with her instructions. Of the greatest importance to this rite was the presence of a white buffalo robe. "Such a robe signified that the spirit being kept was pure, and that all the articles connected with it had been purified."[29]

The association of these rare white robes with the White Buffalo Woman is evident. As Fletcher has indicated, the color white, for the Dakota, generally has the connotation of consecration. Further supporting these linking associations is the fact that "the white Buffalo is rare and generally remains near the center of the herd." This makes it difficult to approach, and therefore it is considered as the Chief or sacred one of the herd. This robe, consequently, is highly prized by the Indian. In accord with the special position of this sacred robe, elaborate ritual details were observed, both in obtaining the animal and preparing the hide.

> [The hide] was purified in the smoke of burning sweet grass. The knife was similarly purified before the animal was skinned, and the hide was removed in such a manner that no blood was shed on it. Only men who had dreamed of animals were allowed to eat any portion of the flesh. . . . The skin was not treated like an ordinary buffalo hide. Only women noted for purity of life could touch or tan it, and after the tanning certain important ceremonies were required. It was the custom for a medicine-man to purify the hide with sweet grass. . . . Even the smallest portion of the robe was a "sacred article."[30]

The crucial role of this bison presence (through the hide which preferably should be white) is completely appropriate and consistent with the larger structuring of Oglala belief. The Oglala see the bison as mother and Earth Principle. This "mother" not only produces and nourishes the temporarily assumed forms of life, but also reabsorbs these forms upon release of the animating powers or spirit which sustained them. Affirmation of this concept can be seen in the fact that the death shroud of a deceased person, placed upon the scaffold, was a bison robe.

In the rites of the purification lodge (the *Inipi*), the Bison is again seen to be present in his skull. This skull was always left with the horns intact, and resided outside the lodge and (usually) to the east of the sacred fire where the rocks were heated. The lodge itself was covered over and sealed by bison robes. In this manner, they too partake of and contribute to the purification function of the rites. Again, an appropriateness of form and concept is indicated. The dome-shaped lodge represents the world or Universe, so the encompassing bison robe is similarly conceived.

The values of purity and ideal womanhood are symbolized by the Buffalo Woman, so the bison is central to the Oglala rites for the consecration of a young girl into womanhood. These rites were referred to by Walker as simply The Buffalo Ceremony. Black Elk used the term *Ishna Ta Awi Cha Lowan* (Preparing for Womanhood). According to an account received from Black Elk, the origin and model for the rites derive from the Lakota, Slow Buffalo (*Tatanka Hunkeshne*), who is said to have had a vision of a buffalo cow cleansing her calf. Through the power of this vision, Slow Buffalo became a holy man (*wichasha wakan*) and understood that he had been given rites which should be used for the benefit of the young women of his nation.

> The Buffalo Ceremony secures for the beneficiary the special care of the Buffalo God, the patron god of chastity, fecundity, industry, and hospitality, the virtues most to be desired of a woman. . . . One for whom this ceremony was performed was called a buffalo woman.[31]

The major features of the ritual complex, as conceived by the Oglala, are as follows:

1. A bison skull with horns is painted and used as an altar. The presiding "Conductor" or medicine man wears a buffalo headdress with the tail trailing at his back.
2. An offering is made of a bundle containing the girl's first menstrual discharge; this offering to the Buffalo God is "placed in a plum tree because it is the emblem of fruitfulness and hospitality preferred by the Buffalo God."
3. The bison skull is purified with tobacco smoke: "My friends we have smoke with the spirit of the buffalo, and the influence of the Buffalo God will be in this lodge."
4. Songs are used which refer to the rutting time of the buffalo bull, and reference is made to the fact that he, the medicine man, is the bull and the girl is a buffalo cow.

5. The medicine man addresses the bison as he paints the skull: "Bull buffalo I have painted your woman's forehead red and have given her a red robe. Her potency is in her horns. Command her to give her influence to this young woman so that she may be a true buffalo woman and bear many children."

6. The medicine man dances, imitating the sounds and movements of the bison, but under the form of the "Crazy Buffalo"; he sidles against the young woman who is protected from the advances by sage placed on parts of her body.

7. Both the medicine man and the woman drink from a bowl on the earth: "We are buffalo on the plains and this is a water hole. The water in it is red for it is sacred and made so by the Buffalo God and it is for buffalo women."

8. Buffalo charms in the form of wands, which had been laid beside the buffalo skull altar, are given to the woman: "These are your Buffalo charms. You should keep them for they will keep bad influences away from you. They have the potency of the Buffalo God and of the spirit of the buffalo. They will keep the two-faced woman, Anogite, from you. They will bring you many children."

9. Throughout the ceremony, the girl is instructed in how to act like a woman, for she is now no longer a girl; finally she is told: "You are akin to the Buffalo God and are His woman. The Buffalo God is pleased with an industrious woman. He is pleased with those who give food to the hungry. . . . You are now a buffalo woman." An eagle plume is tied at the crown of the woman's head, while the medicine man says: "The spirit of the eagle and the duck will be with you. They will give you the influence of the Sun and the South Wind. They will give you many children."

10. In concluding the ceremony, the Conductor states: "You are now a woman. The buffalo woman is your oldest sister. Go out of this lodge." The buffalo skull altar is then turned upside down to indicate the completion of the ceremony.

The rites of the *Hunkapi*, the "Making of Relatives," is also

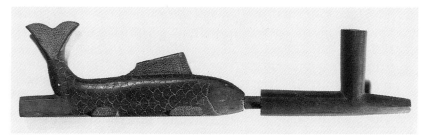

A fish pipe.

considered by the Oglala to be one of the seven rites originally promised by the White Buffalo Cow Woman. The history of these rites is complex, since obviously there have been intrusions of borrowed ritual elements. Among these are the presence of the special "Ree twist tobacco," and rites involving symbolism based on botanical processes in the fertilization of corn. In spite of these intrusions, there are well-integrated core concepts based on lore concerning the bison. This is in complete accord with ancient Lakota patterns. Walker is probably right when he affirms: "The practice of assuming the Hunka relationship has existed among the Lakota since ancient times."[32]

Descriptions of the *Hunkapi* ceremonies indicate the important presence of a bison skull altar. The Buffalo, the patron God of ceremonies, prevailed in the camp. A special portion of meat from the bison is eaten in a sacramental manner by two men (known as *hunkayapi*) between whom a relationship is being established. This relationship was considered to be more binding than that of blood relationships. "This food I shall place in your mouth, so you will never fear my home, for it is your home. In doing this, may *Wakan-Tanka* be merciful to us."[33]

Through this act, there is expressed affirmation of the belief that the Buffalo God caused the spirits of the buffalo to give their meat to the Lakota. When a buffalo was killed for its meat, a portion should be left as an offering to propitiate the spirit. Because this spirit is addressed as *Hunka*, an identity is affirmed between the person known as *hunka* (related) and this interpretation through the words of the medicine man. It would be difficult to find among the Lakota a relationship considered more sacred than that established for the *Hunkayapi*. It is a triangular relationship in which the three actors (two human beings and a bison) are believed to be bound by a common spirit.

An interesting ceremonial detail described by Black Elk is the use of a buffalo ponch sack. The ritual use of this sack follows precisely the pattern used in filling a pipe. The sack is filled, with appropriate prayers addressed to the powers of the six directions. Pinches of tobacco are identified progressively with the West, North, East, South, the Heavens "for the Great spirit," and the Earth: "Grandmother Earth, hear me! Upon you we are making a relationship with a people, just as You have made a relationship with us, by bringing to us our sacred pipe. . . . O Grandmother and Mother, we are placing you in this bag." This sack, now believed to contain the whole Universe, was embraced and kissed in turn by the *hunkayapi*, as well as by all those present at the ceremony.

It could be said with some certainty that the special sacred power attributed to this sack is due, firstly, to the identification of the bison (or bison spirit) with that of the Earth as Mother and Grandmother; and secondly, to the fact that the paunch of the bison is central to the being and itself contains nourishment essential to the animal's life. The sack thus becomes an expression of the Earth Principle. This type of Oglala facility for integrating multiplicity into an aptly symbolized synthesis has been observed in a number of contexts. Indeed, it is generally expressed in the "polysynthetic" character of their language itself.

In the vision quest (*Hanblecheyapi*, "Crying for a Vision"), there is no central focus on the bison. The exception to this can be seen in the sense that through this quest, the individual seeker may enter into contact with the bison spirit. In the formal observances of the Oglala quest, the two possessions which a man may take with him are his pipe and a bison robe. Both of these support the man in that they affirm the presence of the bison spirit. Thus, they affirm the White Buffalo Cow Woman, who it was believed brought the original Pipe to the people.

In the annual rites of the Sun Dance, the role of the bison was, in a sense, secondary to that of the Sun itself. The sun, in this context, was emphasized as the visible source of power and life, and as such was always considered to be an appropriate expression of the Great Spirit. It is important to note the degree to which the bison, and awarenesses of the bison, were integrated into the total complex. It is appropriate that there should be this emphasis on the bison when it is recalled that the Bison People are conceived to dwell under the earth. Nevertheless, they are also "the people of the sun," for the domain of the sun is not only the region above, but also the regions under the world.

Associated with the Sun Dance ceremonies is a "Buffalo Procession," a shaman's buffalo dance, a buffalo feast, and a sacramental feast of buffalo tongues which "should be served so that each one present may have at least a bit of buffalo tongue, for the feast is in honor of and a propitiation to the Buffalo God who is the patron of generosity and hospitality."[34]

The Sun Dancers imitate the buffalo in a special dance which simulates the pawing of a buffalo bull in rage or defiance. Men who dance in this manner for four periods without taking their gaze from the bison head on the central pole may become "Buffalo Men." These dancers are given bison tails on a handle to use as drum beaters. A bison skull must be present as an altar. This skull is painted and the "Mentor" and "Candidate" smoke, alternately blowing the smoke into the nostril cavities of the skull. This should be done in order that the potency of the pipe may harmonize all those communing. A bison head is hung upon the central tree, for the potency of the Buffalo God abides in the head. A rawhide effigy of the bison is also hung on one fork of the tree.

The integration of the bison into the total ritual complex shows the importance of this animal in the lives and values of the people. This is also indicated by the visions of the bison received by the men in the course of the sacrificial "dance." So important are these roles of the bison that he cannot here be considered as secondary to the Sun, but rather as complementary.

The seventh and last rite, *Tapa Wanka Yap* ("The Throwing of the Ball"), was probably a minor ceremonial. Black Elk received the legend from a former "Keeper of the Sacred Pipe," Elk Head. The ceremonial equipment for this rite is very simple. Among the few requirements are a bison skull to be used as an altar. The central ritual implement was a ball made from the hair of the bison and covered with tanned bison hide. This ball was painted red and blue so that "Heaven and Earth were united into one in this ball." The vision which this game-ritual duplicated was received by the Oglala, Moves Walking, who saw the bison teaching the game to a little girl who turned into a buffalo calf, then into a white yearling buffalo, and finally into a larger buffalo. All the bison then turned into people and played the game with the ball of bison hide, throwing it successively to the four directions. At the last throw, straight up into the air, these people again turned into bison. Since they then could no longer play the game, they gave the ball to Moves Walking with the words: "Do not forget that the ball is the world, and also our Father, *Wakan-Tanka*, for the world of the universe is his home; thus, whoever catches the ball will receive a great blessing."

It has been demonstrated in this section that, throughout all the seven major rites, the Bison Principle has been integrated with remarkable pervasiveness and intensity. The Bison was an outstanding representative for most values central to Lakota society, at least those thought of by the people as ideal norms.

The thoroughness with which the Bison has been integrated into Oglala life can, in no small part, be attributed to complex factors rooted in the people's historical–cultural tradition. This, in turn, can be attributed to the stimulus of a multitude of historical interrelationships with other cultures. Yet, the fact remains that the western Lakota history in the Plains is believed not to have exceeded approximately three hundred years. This being the case, the intense enculturation of lore, belief, and ritual activity relating to bison bears witness to the pervasive force with which factors in the environment impinge on the total fabric of a people. The bison was crucial in the people's subsistence economy. Because of this, it is understandable that it was selected out for this role in supporting cultural values. Yet, as has been seen in the important role of the eagle, selectivity need not necessarily be because of subsistence utilization.

Chapter IV
The Metaphysical Nature of Animal Categories in Oglala Lore

The birds and beasts, the trees and rocks, are the work of some great power. Sometimes men say that they can understand the meaning of the songs of the birds. I can believe this is true. They say that they can understand the call and cry of the animals, and I can believe this also is true, for these creatures and man are alike, the work of a greater power . . . we believe that he [Wakan-Tanka] is everywhere.
—Chased by Bears, Lakota

Although Clark Wissler called the trait vague and naive like most primitive ideas, we are grateful to him for drawing attention to the Oglala's mysterious concern with the Whirlwind and the elk. Wissler also pointed out that the concept is not restricted to the elk and the wind in the Oglala mind. It embraces a whole series of unlikely associates. Among these are the bison and bear, the dragonfly, the moth, the cocoon, the spider, and possibly more. That a people can conceive of a perfectly logical interconnection between seemingly disparate phenomena, lends credence to the "prelogical mentality" theories of former times.

In this section, I will reexamine the problem initially exposed by Wissler. By using the conceptual categories of the Oglala himself (thus attempting to see his world as he conceives it),

I hope to clarify the special nature of Oglala magic and its underlying metaphysical basis.

It will be appropriate to commence this analysis with the cocoon, already briefly described in the Introduction. From the cocoon emerges the fluttering butterfly or moth. The cocoon, for the Indian, "is regarded as the bundle or mysterious object from which a power similar to that of the Whirlwind emanates."[1]

The moth, therefore, is conceived as similar to the Whirlwind, because the moth can no more be contained than can the wind. There was believed to be a deep mystery in the wind, since it was intangible and visible only through its effects. Further identification of the moth or butterfly with the "formless" is due to the fluttering actions of the creature's wings, which themselves are wind-producing. This trait, possessed by other winged forms, must also provide access to Whirlwind-power.

The mystery of the relationship is concretized and intensified for the Oglala, through actual possession of a cocoon. A cocoon was often taken with a portion of the twig or surface upon which it was found, wrapped in an eagle plume, and worn on the head. This was regarded as a perpetual prayer to the power of the Whirlwind. Cocoons also were carved in wood by the Sioux. Models of cocoons were made from buckskin, and graphic designs are frequently found. The cocoon-Whirlwind design, for example, was used by Whirlwind Bear in drawing the pictograph of his name.

The cocoon-encapsulated Whirlwind-power is of obvious value to a warrior and hunter. Through processes labeled with unkind connotations as "imitative magic," the individual himself seeks to become intangible, invisible, and destructive like the wind. Having such power, the man, too, would be as difficult to hit as the butterfly or the dragonfly, whom he venerated as having the power to escape a blow. They say the dragonfly cannot be hit by man or animal, nor can the thunder injure it. Hence, the dragonfly is also in touch with a power the Indian covets.

As is typical in the Oglala awareness, there is also inherent in these beliefs a positive–negative polarity. The negative pole to the Whirlwind-power is its power to produce confusion in the mind of the enemy. This was no doubt suggested to the people by the Whirlwind's playful twisting movements. To this end, the Whirlwind in the cocoon is invoked to work its power. In this manner, again in accord with typical Oglala thought processes, the negative is transformed to positive advantage. This point is of special importance in evaluating the quality of Oglala magical beliefs. Unlike more gross forms of magic which may work for the destruction of the opponent, here the power is directed for protective freedom.

The bison also is added to this assembly of cocoon, moth, dragonfly, and butterfly, and tangentially so is the bear. As with most Oglala conceptions, those concerning the bison are based on careful and pragmatic observation. For example, as already described, in winter when a bison cow drops a calf, she is able to blow out from her nose and mouth a red filmy substance which protects the calf, just as the cocoon protects the developing moth. The imagination of the Oglala has also been stimulated by a behavior of the bison bull. When he is pawing the earth, every now and then deftly scooping up the dust and driving it straight into the air, the buffalo is believed to be praying to the Whirlwind to give him power over his enemies.

Graphic illustration of this affinity with Whirlwind-power has been noted on a Gros Ventre ornament. A line is seen connecting the horn of a bison to an insect. This represents a rapport between the buffalo and the moth. These two great powers were considered in sympathy with each other. A double function may be seen to be operative in this dust-throwing trait, for it also has been noted to be used to lure bison cows away from the herd during the rutting season. This attracting power-quality is regarded as especially *wakan* (mysterious/sacred) since among bison it is normally the cow who acts as leader of herds. Similar power over women was especially sought after by young Oglala males. This will be evident in the conceptions described below relating to the elk.

The spider is conceived to be associated with the other beings of our mixed assembly, again through association with the winds. Young spiders send out long filaments which are caught by the wind and which carry these young beings long distances. Further concrete expression is found in the observed fact that certain types of spiders lay out their webs on the ground in rectangular shape with the four corners extended toward the four directions of space. Representation of this form is found repeatedly in Oglala art. Often these works of art have, on the borders of the design, wavy lines representing the power of the Thunders. The association of the spider with the Thunder–Powers can protect and strengthen. These associations may only be understood within the larger context of Oglala mythological belief. In this belief, it is found that the four directions are identified with the "homes" of the four winds, and these winds and their appointed directions are under the control of Thunder-Beings.

The Oglala's magical and practical applications of these forms are based on the fact that the spider's web cannot be destroyed by bullets or arrows. These projectiles pass right through. Further, that as a "friend" of the thunder, the spider or his web has power to protect from harm. The application of these principles is made specific in the custom of stringing up a web-like hammock between four trees, upon which a young child is placed.

The spider is seen as particularly cunning and industrious, traits especially desirable in women. Since his net has the capacity to ensnare, it is conceived that this power may be drawn upon by men in order to attract women to them. Thus, the Oglala courting robe was painted with figures of the spider, as well as with images of the Whirlwind and elk.

The final member to be treated in this assembly of unlikely associates is the elk. The dominant role played by the elk in Oglala values should first be noted. Indication of such strong emphasis is provided in explicit references to a "hypothetical," supernatural Elk. Representation of such spirit animals is indicated by a space in place of a heart. The animal seems to be without a heart, and is thus immortal and supernatural. There seems to be a connection between this opening through the heart and the center of the medicine-hoop, represented by a mirror in the Elk ceremonies. Such belief complexes are associated with the rites of the Oglala Elk festival. In this festival, an elk is painted over the door of the ceremonial tepee in such

A shield (said to have been owned by Crazy Horse).

a manner that all who enter must pass through the body of
the animal.

The characteristics of the elk, utilized by the Oglala for his
magical activities, are based on the mysterious power of the
bull to attract cows to him through his whistling call. This
again represents control over the air or wind principle. The
bull elk, therefore, is seen as the incarnation of the power over
females (a trait highly coveted by the men). The man's further
identity with such power is achieved by simulating the call of
the bull elk with the flageolet. This was thought to draw the

young women of the camp irresistibly to the man playing the instrument.

The Oglala recognized and attempted to utilize the powers which were evidenced in the insects, bison, bear, spider, and elk. This clearly involved psychological processes which were within the realm of imitative and ceremonial magic. As already stated, such magical procedures were nevertheless "innocent" in the sense that they were not projected for the direct harm or destruction of the enemy. Rather, they allowed the individual enemy to have freedom, but to be prevented from the accomplishment of his own aggressive acts. The magic, therefore, is more white than black. Indeed, "black magic" is very rarely utilized by the Oglala and is certainly not sanctioned by the society.

To evaluate this white magic fairly, it must be seen in its total conceptual framework; that is, the Whirlwind principle that was common to the numerous and disparate beings. This Whirlwind (*Umi*) is represented in Oglala mythology as being "unborn," a kind of "playful abstraction from his four brother winds" (*Eya, Yata, Yanpa,* and *Okaga*) who marked the four directions of space. These four winds, with their outcast brother, are all conceived to be the sons of "Tate" and all were born at one time.

According to an Oglala informant, The Four Winds *is* an immaterial God, whose substance is never visible. He is *wakan* and, therefore, no human can comprehend him. While He is one God, he is four individuals. The principle of the four coalesces into a single Wind principle. This qualitatively defined Wind principle cannot be other than the Oglala's *Wakan-Tanka* in which, as the Oglala medicine men have explicitly stated, all *Wakan* beings coalesce, or rather fuse, without becoming confused. It is implied in one of the Oglala legends that "Tate" is "the Great Spirit." In the end, the word *Wakan-Tanka* includes all the *Wakan* beings, because they are all as if one.

Behind expressions that may appear to be naive to the outside observer, there is a depth of thought. This very thought successfully links and integrates a multiplicity of forms within a more general and unifying conception. The Oglala conceive the horizontal dimension of the world of appearances as being intercepted with the vertical dimension of the sacred. In this point, or moment of intersection, the sense of mystery is apprehended.

Chapter V
The Power of Sacred Animals in Oglala Art

The first and foremost perspective to establish here is that traditional arts (and this must always include crafts) express through external forms that which is most internal, or spiritually central, to the individuals of the particular culture.

If traditional art forms constitute vehicles that bear a people's most sacred values, such expressions are precious documentations for remembering values which may have been neglected or lost under the pressures of a contemporary world increasingly motivated by very different priorities. Indeed, with North American Indian groups, the traditional art forms, including the ritual or liturgical arts, have often been instrumental in the reconstitution or revitalization of traditional values and related life-ways.

The rich languages of the traditional arts of primal peoples constitute a range of spiritual perspectives and fundamental assumptions which today are continually partially or totally misunderstood. The following is a brief clarification of at least the central perspectives.

Within created traditional forms there can be no dichotomy between arts and crafts. First of all, art is not the particular created form, but the inner principle by or from which the outer form comes into being. To dismiss utilitarian items as being "only crafts" is, through ignorance or ill will, a modern prejudice. This prejudice has contributed to the tragic separation of art from life and to a presiding cult which glorifies the banal and passing idiosyncrasies of human individuals over the affirmation of universal and timeless realities.

A fundamental perspective latent to the spoken languages of primal peoples is that the word or name mysteriously makes present the essence or power of what is named. This power is enhanced by the understanding that speech is borne by the breath, and breath comes from the area of the heart that is understood as the spiritual center of the living being. Equally, traditional art forms are experienced not just as symbols of some other agreed-upon referent. A spiritual essence of power specific to the particular form is present in an immediacy of experience. For example, an animal or a vision-being painted on a shield or the cover of a lodge is understood to be really present with the fullness of its particular spiritual powers which may be transmitted to the observer.

Visual Representations of Animals and Birds

Paralleling this primal concept of language, and of the word not as "symbol" but as an immediate event, is the quality of experiencing the visual arts and crafts. I should stress first of all that for primal peoples generally there is no dichotomy between the arts and crafts, in the manner that our art historians insist on, where art is one kind of thing that can be placed on a mantelpiece or hung on the wall, and the craft item is inferior because it is made for utilitarian ends. This seems to me a most artificial distinction and I think it is time that we outgrew it. . . . Native American life-ways are of technical excellence and are also beautiful. They must be made in special sacred ways, and the materials of the tools and objects made have to be gathered with prayer and offerings. Beauty and truth are here one![23]

Representations of animal and bird forms were produced by the Oglala through infrequent carvings in wood, musical implements (flutes and whistles), rawhide cutouts (the bison), quill work, stuffed amulet figures (turtle and lizard), engravings on bison horn, and occasionally red-stone pipes. Representations of animals, however, were most frequently

Bison pictograph on cave wall.

depicted on the many types of Oglala hide paintings. This demonstrated an understanding of the essential quality of the form, as well as a highly developed aesthetic sensitivity for line, space, and color. This graphic skill was also applied to the depiction of Winter Counts, personal name pictographs, records of personal war exploits on "ghost screens" of the warriors' lodges, tepee paintings, parfleche designs, decorations on clothing (shirts, ,robes, dresses, and accessories), body paints, and the protective medicine-paintings on shields. Although animal and bird forms were depicted, it should be emphasized that many of the Oglala art forms were not of living beings, but rather were abstract and geometric designs.

Probably the most comprehensive collection of Teton Dakota animal paintings appeared on the Sacred Pipe tepee that was destroyed in Berlin during World War I. Fortunately, it was described in great detail and with excellent illustrations by Friederich Weygold in 1903. Of the approximately one-hundred

An eagle spoon.

figures painted on this tepee, the majority were birds and animals. The few paintings that did not directly depict animals were in some way related to them. Even the central motif of the "Sun-burst" and the sacred pipe were depicted with wings, and both have been noted as being related to the bison.

Regrettably, no account exists of an Indian's own interpretation of this tepee with its painted forms. The importance for the people of such a painted tepee and of the animals displayed on it suggested that humans never had the right to paint medicine-animals unless they had received visions or dreams of such beings. The paints themselves were considered to have their own inherent powers. Such medicine-paints were carefully prepared from particular types of earth and mixed with special herbs. It has even been noted that certain colors, specifically red or vermillion, were obtained through a special firing process. Certain colors had associations with the powers of the four directions, which were symbolically presided over by specific birds. These colors, for the Oglala, were usually black (or blue-black) for the West, white for the North, red for the East, and yellow for the South. Red and sometimes green were also associated with the earth.

Especially notable among the animals depicted on the Pipe tepee was an example of a Thunderbird, represented with an opening or hollow where its heart would be. A key to understanding this is provided in the statements from an Oglala source in reference to the mythical or archetypal elk.

> The conception seems to be, that an animal without a heart is immortal and supernatural; at least, this is the way in which the mythical elk was described. According to the belief, there is a connection between the opening through the heart and the center of the medicine-hoop, represented in the elk ceremonies by the mirror.[24]

A similar sacred medicine-hoop, attached by ,a zigzag power-line to the wing of a horned Thunder-being, is also depicted on the Pipe tepee.

One example of a painted bison robe, which also focuses on the importance given by the Oglala to the elk, is a "courting blanket" described by Wissler:

> The figure of a woman was the main part of the design with

zigzag lines extending from the nostrils of the elk around the
woman, connecting with the head of the spider. . . . These lines
indicate the direction of the power toward the woman, and that
she is enveloped by it.[25]

The description of elk, spider, and Whirlwind in Chapter II
should clarify the ideas involved in this particular robe
painting.

Stylized animals painted on the bodies of men were of a
different type from the graphic painting described above.
Nevertheless, the common use of these imaginative designs
and the identification process which this custom suggests indicate the importance of presenting at least three animal
examples. In accord with a vision received of the spider, Black
Elk is seen depicted in a photograph with the body of the
spider painted in yellow on his chest. The paired legs of the
spider extend along both of Black Elk's arms and down both
legs. Wissler has mentioned that members of the Wolf Society
painted a coyote image on their bodies before going on a
warpath. To assure effective transfer of the power of the
medicine-paints and the image itself, the painting had to be
executed by a medicine man or someone instructed by such a
person.

> A broad red band across the mouth and cheeks, and a vertical
> red mark across each eye. The idea is the bloody mouth of the
> coyote when feeding. The four coyote skin bearers paint the
> face over with blue and scratch it down with the finger tips.
> These marks are said to denote that their medicine is strong;
> they are also credited with power to induce storms and fogs to
> conceal them from enemies.

Charles Long Rock, an Oglala, mentioned a painting of yellow
with dark blue across the eyes and figures like deer horns
extending from the corners of the mouth. This form of painting
was taught him by the medicine man.

Among those eminently sacred forms painted by the Oglala,
there must be special reference to the devices and designs
depicted on shields. Their bold simplicity and spontaneous
mode of execution make these paintings very different in style
from the more sophisticated war records. It might be said that

it is difficult to find examples anywhere of more virile and imaginative art.

This quality is undoubtedly due to the dominating motivation in these designs. This motivation was to crystallize the essence of the vision or dream experience. No animal or bird was excluded from possession of such protective powers. The underlying protective principle might be specific to an experience known only to the recipient. Verbal interpretation of the painted form may be impossible for the bearer himself. Wissler refers to a shield painting possessed by an old man who did not know the meaning of the designs painted on his shield. In his experience, no instructions were given. This was of little importance, since he always felt the peculiar supernatural presence of the sacred forms which expressed his experience. In other words, it was believed that the painted device *in itself* possessed the desired power-quality, and its operational effectiveness did not require the secondary interpretation of the human agency. However, the power contained in the painting usually had to be correctly "activated" through established ceremonial procedure, song, or prayers. The magical mode of operation of these shields has been made explicit in a statement received by Frances Densmore from an old Lakota Warrior:

> The decoration on the shield was said to refer to a dream of a bear. The eight segments were painted alternately red and yellow, the painting on the yellow segments, in black, representing bears' paws, while the space below the paws was white. The warrior said that the decoration commemorated a fight with the Crows, and that certain features of the painting showed that the fight, though in the Black Hills, took place in a level open place. He said that he was "in the middle of the shield and the enemies were all around him, but the claws of the bear were on every side to protect him, hence he was not hurt in the battle."[27]

An important dimension in Lakota statements concerning the protective powers of medicine-shields is that in all of these conceptions, we find less appeal to the deities for the direct destruction of enemies than for a shielding protection to enable the *man himself* to be the destructive agent. These protective powers have been called "magical," but the term should be "religio-magical." Such qualification indicates the operating presence of principles which transcend the domain of magic. At the very least, they indicate more strongly religious and positive connotations than those which are generally connected with this term.

We have seen that the Oglala paintings of sacred, protective animals have their original model in the vision experience. It may also be said that there is a retroactive process of intensification operating here which tends to be self-perpetuating. That is, graphic display of an aspect of a vision experience, no matter how abstract or stylized, tends to condition and orient other individuals for a similar quality experience. An example of this was noted for the vision enactment through dance ceremonials.

There is a quality of understanding and participation on the part of these people that cannot be sufficiently described in terms limited to the aesthetic or to the realm of emotion. This material indicates the presence of intellectual and spiritual dimensions which transcend the levels of the aesthetic and emotional experience.

Some Examples of Images

In viewing traditional art forms, particularly those of primal peoples, the tendency is to dissociate the human agent or artisan who originally created the form from the created object itself, thus missing an essential spiritual element. Neither beauty nor truth can manifest itself, at least in human mode, except through a being who has realized the sacred realities within himself or herself. The portraits of Plains people on the following pages speak to the quality of such realization.

In order to understand the artifacts of primal peoples fully and deeply, one must realize that the human agent is an aspect of the message, and the elements of the natural environment of the culture play a quasi-determining role.

Every part of the bison is used not only for sustenance, but also in the creation of almost everything necessary to the Plains Indians' nomadic life. For this reason the bison is associated with totality, the universe, and is considered a provider of almost all of life's needs.

Black Elk.

Lame Bull.

White Buffalo.   *Wolf Head.*

Suzie Yellowtail.

Chief Wolf Robe.

Little Warrior

In a similar manner, the land itself, in all its beauty and bounty, is understood as a mother to the people, also providing everything that is essential to the lives of the people. As with all primal arts, little attempt is made to achieve naturalistic representation. On a painted deerskin robe, for example it is not a particular horse that is depicted, but a universalized horse, the essence of horse.

The totality of all the animals of the Plains Indian environment, each with its specific qualities, spells out a totality of differentiated essential values which were integrated into the peoples' lives and culture.

The Tepee

This nineteenth-century drawing shows the typical dwelling of the once nomadic Plains Indian, the tepee. It is an example of sacred architecture since the conical dwelling is understood as an image of the world or universe with the supporting poles linking heaven and earth. The tepee poles reach upward as if to bring down powers from the heavens into the dwelling,

A Blackfoot "Yellow Buffalo Tepee" from Montana, circa 1900.

and the fire at the center of the lodge is the presence of "The Great Mysterious," the ultimate principle. One tepee had the image of a bison encircling the dwelling in such a manner that its midsection was positioned over the doorway. Thus, in entering, one became ritually identified with the bison. As with all sacred arts of the Plains, the owner of the lodge had earned the right to this particular bison motif through his personal sacred vision experience received in a lonely retreat while fasting and suffering. Living in such a dwelling is to participate continually in a liturgy, the most powerful of the sacred arts.

In a similar manner, the owner of another lodge received sacred powers through the otter which was depicted above the doorway, while the images on a Cheyenne tepee of the late nineteenth century told that the owner was a sacred pipe bearer who through his powers had obtained many horses.

It is interesting to note the contrast between the sacred conical/circular tepees and the contemporary square-wall tents. The old people always said that there was no power in the square, only in the circle. But in the contemporary canvas tepee, the "smoke flaps" can be adjusted with the long poles so that there is hardly ever any smoke within the lodge.

Clothing

Men's shirts were made from deer hide, a sign of how the animal was respected. The skin of the legs was left intact; indeed, almost none of the hide was cut. Such garments constitute a sacred and liturgical art, and to wear such a shirt was to incorporate into oneself the qualities or powers latent to this particular animal.

The fringes on the garments speak of the sacred powers which radiate out from a sacred source, in this case the deer and also the human being. Images of pipes on a Cheyenne shirt from Wyoming indicated that the wearer was probably a Keeper of Sacred Pipes. Hair fringes on such shirts are often incorrectly associated with scalp-locks taken in warfare. In fact, they were more often special shirts belonging to recognized leaders of band groups, the hair being that of close relatives who supported the young leader.

An example of porcupine quill embroidery on a smoked buckskin.

Quilled containers were made by the women to contain a person's most sacred possession: the tobacco smoking-pipe. Elongated fringes on these containers, or on any other objects, always refer to the presence of sacred power. Porcupine-quill embroidery on smoked buckskin was a most important and particularly sacred women's craft.

In the mythology of all Plains peoples, the porcupine, which climbs high into trees, is associated with the Sun and the creative principle, its quills therefore being identified with the Sun's rays. Such legends are held very closely by the women. Those who work with the quills are organized into guilds or secret societies, and never divulge the mysteries of their craft.

Men's robes were made from the hide of bison bulls and were appropriately decorated with "sun-burst" symbols which express the male generative principle. The "sun-burst" motif often contained the central cross-hatched figure of a stylized sunflower, a flower which during the day always turns to face the sun, the Source of Life. This movement is imitated by the participants in the annual Spring Sun Dance ceremonies of the Lakota Sioux. The double-triangle figures radiating out from the center are the feathers and plumes of the eagle, a solar

A dress from the early 1800s decorated with porcupine quills. Quillwork was a very special and sacred craft.

being, and symbolize the life-giving rays of the sun. The same symbol is also a representation of a cocoon which contains the potential living form to be released: a moth or butterfly. The entire figure speaks of both the creative force of the Ultimate Principle (The Great Mysterious – *Wakan-Tanka* in Lakota), and also of all Potentiality.

The women's robes were made from hides of the bison cow and decorated with abstract representations of the feminine reproductive and life forces rather than the solar symbols used on the men's robes.

A design common to diverse types of art expressions of the Americas, and often referred to by the unfortunate term "X Ray motif" looks behind the outer layers of illusory or lesser realities, the "appearances," and into the inner spiritual Essence or Principle which is universal to all phenomena. It is through understandings of such depth that the interrelatedness of all life is seen as a presiding principle of Native American peoples.

On this shield a grizzly bear offers protection by extending its paw toward oncoming arrows and stopping them.

Artifacts

A genre of particularly powerful men's paintings are those found on the protective circular shields made from the heat-tempered hide of the bison bull. The painted motif typically originates from a vision experience received during a many-day spiritual retreat and total fast. The painted sacred being is understood to be really present in its image, and lends its powers to protect the bearer from the arrows or bullets of the enemy. An example would be the image on a shield whose owner received powers from the spider. The spider's power is symbolized by the zigzag lines extending from the head of the being.

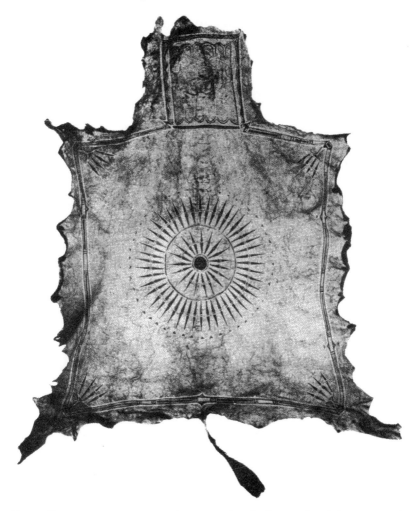

Sacred powers were not just received through vision experiences of the past. Lakota artist Arthur Amiotte, grandson of Standing Bear, is an example of today's younger leaders who are continuing and revitalizing the sacred traditions not only of the Plains peoples, but also of many tribal groups of North America. Today's artists must use available materials, but portions of the work are still done with sacred porcupine quills, buckskin, and beadwork.

The Sun-Burst on a buffalo hide is a reminder of the great liturgical arts of the Plains peoples, the annual spring "Sun Dance" ritual, a ceremony of great beauty and dignity. It takes place within a circular lodge understood as the world or Universe with a sacred tree at the center as the axis joining heaven and earth. For three or four days and nights the participants fast and suffer within the lodge. They dance almost continuously to the rhythm of large drums and powerful songs, moving with dignified steps to the central tree and then backwards to their places at the periphery, but always facing the Center.

Special prayers are offered at each sunrise, and songs of great antiquity bless the sun, all the powers of the Universe, and all life. These profound ceremonies (and there are hundreds more with equal depth) continue today not only among the Plains peoples, but also among many other tribal groups of North America. It is a presiding belief that if the myths, sacred tales, rites, and ceremonies are abandoned, the cycle of the world will come to an end.

Three Drawings

The next three figures have been reproduced from very small plates of inferior quality which originally appeared in Clark Wissler's article on Oglala Societies, printed in the *Anthropological Papers of the American Museum of Natural History* (1912). The original drawings, probably made by an Oglala Sioux, are in the collection of R. Cronau. The author expresses his gratitude to Ann Parker for her skillful and faithful reproduction of these fine Indian drawings.

This drawing represents the ceremonial dance of the Elk Dreamer's Society and depicts its members' magical affiliation with the Elk's power. Only the two dancers carrying "elk hoops" and directly caught up in the Elk's power belong to the Elk cult; the other dancers belong to the Buffalo and the Black-Tail Deer Cult respectively. The fact that the woman holding the pipe also has a forked stick and is connected to the Black-Tail Deer dancer with the power-line issuing from the Elk, suggests that she may be the mythical "Two-Face" or "Double-Woman."

In this detail from an Elk Dance, the breath-whistle ("bugle") of the Elk is depicted. The hoops carried and supported by the dancer have circular mirrors (the Elk's heart) supported by spider webs. Note the depiction of the Pipe in both this figure and the previous one. The Pipe here undoubtedly shows the symbolic breath–wind principle involved in the rite of smoking. The association of a black bird (raven) with the elk's foot is not clear to the author.

This drawing represents the mystical power of the bull Elk over the cow; the presence of the "elk hoop" and central mirror is again noted.

Conclusion

It is appropriate to conclude this section with one of Ananda Coomaraswamy's brief and always succinct statements, written as part of the introduction to a book on the chantways of the *Dine*, or Navajo Indians of the Southwest:

> The most immediate significant point is that of the artist's priestly or ministerial function. The original intention of intelligible form was not to entertain us but literally to remind us. The chant is not for the approval of the ear or the picture for that of the eye (although these senses can be taught to approve the splendor of truth, and can be trusted when they have been trained), but to affect such a transformation of our being as is the purpose of all ritual acts.
>
> It is, in fact, the ritual arts that are the most artistic because they are the most correct, as they must be if they are to be effectual.

Chapter VI
We Are All Related

> *The elements and majestic forces in nature, lightning, wind,*
> *fire, and frost, were regarded with awe as spiritual powers,*
> *but always secondary and intermediate in character. We*
> *believed that the spirit pervades all creation.*
> —Charles A. Eastman (*Ohiyesa*), Dakota

This book has attempted to define the range of resources utilized by a nomadic hunting people. I have collated the conceptions that these peoples hold toward certain important animals and birds within their habitat, and demonstrated that this focus yields a rich range of values which contribute to a more detailed and comprehensive knowledge. This study has examined the modes by which these types of ideas, values, and religious beliefs become integrated within areas of the socio-cultural fabric. This latter emphasis serves to define awarenesses with greater clarity. Above all, this book provides an index of the frequency and intensity with which elements of an external natural environment impact upon a culture. In this study, clarification of religious type has resulted, which interrelates and interacts with factors selected out of the natural environment.

It cannot be assumed that this book has exhausted the total range of inherent possibilities. Forms out of the habitat, which may be selected by a people, are of an indefinite number. So are the culturally conditioned subjective interpretations of such forms. Available data is incomplete. Individuals are only able to express certain aspects within the fabric of the culture. Finally, the observers represent their own specific predetermined concerns. These concerns, in turn, affect their perceptions.

By isolating preselected components of a culture, and by focusing on these, there is a risk of distortion. This distortion occurs by presenting an unbalanced view of the actual psycho-cultural situation. By selecting out the faunal and avian beings for exposition of a people's belief, an almost pathological obsession with these particular forms is implied. This excludes other potential points of emphasis within the range of the people's total world of experience. In this world of the Lakota, attention was also directed to the "inanimate" elements of the habitat. Notwithstanding, it is safe to conclude that the presiding focus on animals is representative for the Oglala. This is to be expected, given the economic subsistence core of a nomadic hunting culture. These perspectives have been well defined by Ivar Paulson:

> To be sure, the structure and morphology of the sacred embraces the entire area between heaven and earth which is experienced by man. But because of a very natural mental outlook which is determined by the particular dominant interest of a specific ecotype, it comes to be experienced in more circumscribed sectors of the natural environment.[1]

The Unifying Power of the Wind

It has been seen that the Oglala tended to group or link phenomena in terms of interconnections based on the receptivity manifested by certain kinds of beings. This was noted in such seemingly disparate companions as the bison, elk, bear, dragonfly, moth, cocoon, and spider. Undoubtedly, the series could be extended indefinitely with a shifting of levels of abstraction, which is possible in relation to the character of the unifying principle operating here. This point will be clarified below. The above grouping of beings seems to defy explanation in non-Indian classification. The connecting principle, in the Oglala mind, is evident in the observed and obvious fact that all these beings are the favored recipients of a specific kind of invisible power. This power is unified in itself, but may operate in diverse ways.

A Sioux buffalo skin.

It was these kinds of manifested qualities that the Indian
intended to acquire for himself; to be as swift and as difficult
to hit as the dragonfly; to be as invulnerable to bullets or
arrows as the spider's web; to have the attracting power over
the opposite sex as does the elk, or to be as free as the Whirlwind nurtured in the cocoon. These qualities can be acquired
by the individual if he can establish a kind of "receptive identity" with the form manifesting the desired quality.

The unifying power underlying these disparate forms was
seen to be the wind or whirlwind, represented as *Umi*. That
the moth had access to this power was evident in its wind-
creating wings, and the cocoon was the container of this

potential wind-power. The spider had access to this power because his ensnaring net stretches out to the four directions, which are conceived as the home of the four winds. The bison had the wind-power which he employed for his own purposes; while the elk's particular utilization of this wind-power was witnessed in his ability to "whistle" in such a manner that cows were attracted to him.

In theory, the components of this complex web of direct and indirect associations may be multiplied indefinitely in the Indian's thought processes. There is no living creature whose life does not ultimately depend on the presence of the wind, conceived as breath. In this perspective, breath has been fixed upon as a symbol of the life principle.

It is important to the ideas being defined here to clarify the essential nature of the rites of smoking and the manner in which the animal beings are integrated. In the smoking of the pipe, both the "horizontal" dimension of relationship and the "vertical" dimension of identity are affirmed. Relationship is established by the fact that all who smoke together participate in the same ritual and in the same prescribed ritual movements. In these rites, the relationship is extended to include the powers of the four directions of space, the homes of the four controlling winds. These controlling winds are conceived as one power in their father, the wind, who dwells in the sky. To this principle, the pipe stem is pointed to the four directions and, afterwards, to the sky. In the process of doing this, it is said "I smoke with the Great Spirit;" and in terminating the rites of smoking, all participants say *mitaku oyasin*, "we are all related." In the smoking rites, the proper concept of relationship merges with the concept of identity. As grains of tobacco are placed in the bowl of the pipe, they are identified with the names of birds and animals. Indeed, all powers and forms of creation are mentioned. The filled pipe thus becomes a comprehensive and synthetic totality, and all forms are merged and unified with the addition of fire.

It has been necessary to extend statements of the Oglala's orientation toward unification beyond specific examples. It is only within the larger context that the ultimate quality of the relationship that exists with the animals and birds may be fully realized. The best reference we have to these "ultimate" types of concepts came from men of exceptional character, medicine men such as Finger, Sword, and Black Elk.

Animal Guardians and Metamorphosis

Evidence shows that the Oglala's structuring of phenomena represents a type of cognitive organization and orientation that is very different from that of the non-Indian. Areas of Oglala values and ideas which have been presented in this text are found in conceptions and beliefs concerning types of animal guardians. To the Oglala, the animal-guardian-spirit concept is the reality of the dream and vision experience. It is also related to metamorphosis.

Comparison of these formulations with the highly developed and structured experience of the eastern woodland peoples are nominally present, found only in the bison. Such an expression of Bison as "Master Guardian" is found through informants who cite the belief in a Buffalo God.

This Master-Bison has control over the game and over a number of mythological formulations. This view is really a more generalized concept, in which the bison represents all growing and living things upon the earth. There are statements among the Oglala of no other Master-Guardian animals. The exception might be that, of the birds of the air, the eagle is Chief. But this role is to be understood in an exclusively spiritual sense. The polarity expressed here is significant and typical of Oglala awareness and values. The Oglala may have had such beliefs in relation to the bear, or to other animals, but we have no recorded information to validate this.

In determining whether values do indicate the function of "guardianship," it is important to distinguish beliefs in animal guardians from those in Spirit-animals or archetypes. The latter seem to refer to functions of guardianship, but distinction between the two concepts is very difficult to establish. The general Dakota belief is that each class of animal or object of like kind possesses a peculiar guardian divinity which is the mother archetype, the Archetype concept being central to Oglala belief. The pattern is so well established that it is safe to assume that in Oglala belief, all animals and birds have their "spirit-Archetypes" which assume the appearance of the respective phenomenal being.

As noted above, it is very difficult to distinguish between concepts involving the Animal Guardians and the Spirit-Animals. It is especially difficult to establish which of the above is implied in the Guardian Spirit which appears in the individual's vision quest. Sword's definition of the *Nagiya* seems to fit with all the explicit and implicit statements received from the Oglala about the Guardian Spirit. The *Nagiya* are the immaterial selves of material things, and these immaterial selves seem to describe qualities of the archetypal principle. Thus, the *Nagiya* of a bear may possess a man when the man wants to have the nature of a bear. The Spirit-animal may or may not take on the role of animal guardian. In its appearance to man, however, emphasis is placed on the qualitative nature of the power. This, then, is translated into at least three possible categories of qualities: (1) those desirable in warfare; (2) those affirming ideal patterns of behavior or character; and (3) the acquisition of purely spiritual understanding. All three have been documented in this book.

Due to variations in individual experience, the precision with which the nature of the Guardian Spirit may be defined is a question still to be answered. This search is of value, for otherwise we are left with the unsatisfactory stand of Lowie, who abandoned the matter to no more than the pluralistic realm of "thrill." The intellectual or spiritual dimension expressed and experienced by the people is worthy of more serious consideration.

Further example of the Oglala's structuring of experience is seen in the frequency of incidents in which metamorphosis is expressed. Both mythic statement and vision experience express the reality of such "phenomenal" change, and both are mutually self-supporting. Legends tell of a boy and the hero turning into hawks; of human beings becoming mountain lions; of a grandmother turning into a crazy buffalo, and so on. Numerous such examples could be presented.

In other words, there is a belief in a gradation, or at least a distinction, in what are conceived to be very "real" spiritual animal beings underlying their physical forms. Finally, there is widespread belief in the possibility of human metamorphosis into animals. Further examples could be given, but through these that have been stressed, there is evidence of a quality of cognitive orientation and a structuring of phenomena very different from that of the non-Indian.

The Oglala have an ability to organize categories of power or phenomena into generalized sets. Nevertheless, there is projected here a world with less rigid limits than the one experienced by the non-Indian. There is a fluidity and transparency to their perceptions of the world which permit no absolute line to be drawn. For example, no clear line is drawn between the worlds of animals, men, or spirits. Outward forms are conceived to be shifting, and some may be receptive and dangerous. Alien dichotomies of the natural as against the supernatural hold little validity when applied to this type of world perception. Time itself takes on the nature of a non-fragmented continuum. This world of the Lakota, however, is neither unstructured nor chaotic, for underlying the fluidity of appearances there is the binding thread of the *Wakan* concept. An ultimate coalescence of the multiple into the unifying principle of *Wakan-Tanka* does not compromise an essential unity. The world of the Oglala is seen to be a spiritualized world in which the phenomenal is rigorously affirmed for what it is. This affirmation is never dissociated from underlying principles.

The Interrelationships of Man, Culture and Environment

This study has dealt with a range of forms in a specified habitat. It has examined the types of interactions between the environment and the culture of its people. In these interrelationships, it is evident that the historical and cultural traditions always play an important role. This role determines which forms are to be selected by the people, how they are to be utilized, and what will be the nature of the values affixed onto the phenomenal forms. Remember always that culture is born within individuals. Nevertheless, it is impossible to speak of environmental determinism as operating here in an unqualified manner. Between these theories of environmental

A horned-elk spoon.

determinism and historico-cultural determinism, there must be some middle ground. It is this middle ground which calls for definition in this book.

In dealing with the data, I have been particularly impressed with two facts. The first is the appropriateness which exists between form and function. In terms of tools, clothing, dwellings, and the entire range of subsistence needs, there have been adjustments and modifications. From porcupine quills to the uncut bison robe, there has occurred a transference that is apt, efficient, and satisfying in terms of man's total needs.

The second impressive fact is the extraordinary aptness with which values, crystalized in belief and concept, are associated with the selected resources of the environment. So fitting are these relationships, it is as if the forms or beings were themselves the initiating agents for the concepts. Nothing seems to have been forced arbitrarily to make the idea fit the form. The correspondences between levels of reality are as if one were the reflection of the other; they flow into each other in a manner that expresses a totally integrated environment.

The evidence points to the following conclusions. There is a set of triadic relationships in which all members—man, culture, and the natural environment—interrelate and interact, each with its own quality of input. The nature of the roles of the environmental forms cannot be excluded as a creative, promotive element in this triadic process which, in an ultimate sense, cannot be conceived outside of Man.

Appendix A
The Oglala and Siouan Speaking Groups

The term "Sioux" seems to have been derived from a French-Canadian abbreviation of the Chippewa diminutive term *Nadowe-is-iw-ug*, meaning "they are the lesser adders" and thus "enemies." The term is therefore one of some derision and has never been used among the "Sioux" themselves. The term "Siouan," however, has come to refer exclusively to that very large linguistic family comprising the following groups: Assiniboin, Crow, Hidatsa, Iowa, Kansa, Mandan, Missouri, Omaha, Osage, Oto, Ponca, Quapaw, Santee, Yankton, and Teton.

The term "Dakota" ("allied" or "kindred"), or "Dakota Sioux," as has been commonly used, refers to a large grouping of seven bands or "Council Fires" (*Oceti-Sakowin*), which are grouped into three divisions: the Eastern Santee, the Middle or *Wioiyela*, and the Western Division. The Eastern Santee, who speak the Dakota dialect, are comprised of the Mdewakantonwan, the Wahpekute, the Sisitonwan or Sisseton, and the Wahpetonwan or Wahpeton. The Middle Division, speaking the *Nakota* dialect, are the Yankton and the Yanktonai. The largest Western Division, speaking the Lakota dialect, are the Titowan or Teton.

The Western Teton Division is further subdivided into the following sub-bands, the locations indicated being those of their present reservations:

1. The *Oglala* (Scatter their Own) of Pine Ridge Reservation, South Dakota, with some families living on the Rosebud Reservation
2. The *Sicango* (Burnt Thighs thus Brulé) who live on the Rosebud Reservation, South Dakota, with a few families living on Pine Ridge

3. The *Itazipco* (without Bows, thus Sans Arcs) who live on the Cheyenne River Reservation, South Dakota
4. The *Sihasapa* (Black Foot) who live on both the Cheyenne River Reservation and the Standing Rock Reservation in North and South Dakota
5. The *Minikondzu* or *Minnekonjou* (Plant Beside the River) who live on the Cheyenne River Reservation, South Dakota
6. The *Oohennonpa* (Two Kettles) who also live on the Cheyenne River Reservation
7. The *Hunkapapa* (Campers at the Horn, or End, or the Camping Circle) who live on Standing Rock Reservation, North and South Dakota, with some families living on the Wood Mountain reservation No. 160, Saskatchewan.

All these seven sub-bands of the Western Teton speak the Lakota dialect, and refer to themselves by this term.

Appendix B
Uses of the Bison

Part of Animal	Usage
Horns	Spoon ladles
	Wedges for splitting
	Tips, used in game
	Curing blood diseases
	Headdresses
	Bloodsucking cups
	Scrapers, with blade inserted
	Bow manufacturing
Hide (raw)	Parflech containers
	Bull Boat
	Rattles
	Glue
	Mortar, shaped round for pounding
	Shield
	Ropes, lariats
	Cases for sacred medicines
	Death Sheet for deceased
	Saddle manufacturing
	Other horse gear
	Drumheads
	Snowshoes
Hides (tanned)	Robes, for winter use
	Covers for tepees
	Moccasins, loincloths
	Wrapping for the deceased
	Bedding
	War deeds, painted on
	Disguise for hunting bison

Part of Animal	Usage
Hides (tanned)	Tepee floor covering
	Pouches, multiple types
Hair/Fur	Halters, reatas, horse gear
	Moccasin stuffing (when cold)
	Saddle padding
	Balls for children's games
	False hair
	Brushes for painting
	Stuffing for dolls, pillows, and so on
	Decoration on armlets, belts, and so on
Bone	Needles
	Cylinders for decoration
	Arrow points
	Sled runners
	Knives
	Awls for sewing
	Bull-roarer
	Spades
	Tanning process
	Tools for thinning hides
Paunch	Water containers
	Cooking, boiling water
	Keeping innards
Bladder	Tobacco containers
	Water containers
Scrotum	Rattles
Sinew	Handles for small tools
	Arrow points
	Backing for bows
	Bow strings
	Thread for sewing
	Ropes, cordage, bindings
	Glue manufacturing
Tripe	Buckets and food storage
Tail	War club
	Water switch in steam bath
Hoof	Hatchet or mallet for butchering
	Glue
	Rattles and pendants

Part of Animal	*Usage*
Intestines	Sack for keeping innards
	Sausage manufacturing
	Water bags
Blood	Smeared on arrows for greater penetration
Tallow	Healing wounds
	Sealing tobacco in pipes
	Mixed with paints
	Weaning children
Gristle	Glue
	Chewed by teething babies
Heart	Bag from inner lining
Dung ("chips")	Fuel
	To prevent chafing of babies
	Burned as incense
	Arrow targets

Ceremonial and Ritual Uses

Bladder	With pemmican, offering with deceased
Chips	To rest pipe on
	Mixed with tobacco for lighting pipes
	Burned for incense
Fur	Shed hair tied on head as remembrance of the coming of the White Buffalo Maiden
	Hair ornament worn in Sun Dance
	Worn by "Intercessor" in Sun Dance
Hide (tanned)	Displayed on pole with scalplock
	Ceremonial complex (White Bison hide)
	Given or left as offering
	Worn by Sun Dance leader
	Robes for men in Sun Dance
	Robes for wrapping the dead
Hide (raw)	Effigies of man and bison for Sun Dance
	Sacrificial ropes for Sun Dance
Heart	Fat from heart to seal pipe

Appendix C
Qualities Associated with Animals

	Bison	Elk	Deer	Bear	Badger	Gopher	Skunk	Wolf	Fox	Rabbit
Feminine Powers										
Earth, Creativity	x			x	x					
Feminine virtues	x									
Hospitality	x									
Generosity	x									
Gentleness									x	x
Humility										x
Feminine courage	x								x	
Power over males			x							
Cocoon creating	x									
Masculine Powers										
Strength	x	x		x	x			x		
Courage	x	x		x			x	x	x	
Persistence	x	x		x	x		x		x	
Defender	x	x								
Invulnerability	x			x						
Invisibility								x		

	Bison	Elk	Deer	Bear	Badger	Gopher	Skunk	Wolf	Fox	Rabbit
Swiftness		x	x					x	x	x
Observation				x				x	x	
Attentiveness								x	x	
Terrifying aspects				x		x				
Power over females	x	x								
Wind Powers										
Whirlwind	x	x		x						
Confusing the enemy	x			x				x		
Ambivalent attitudes			x	x						
Metamorphosis	x		x	x						
Curing Powers	x			x	x			x		
Ability to find things				x	x					
A Species Chief	x									
Spiritual Archetype	x	x		x				x		

	Turtle	Serpent	Eagle	Hawk	Crow	Owl	Lark	Dragonfly	Moth	Spider
Feminine Powers										
Earth principle	x	x					x			x
Feminine virtues, Power	x						x			x
Gentleness						x	x			
Cocoon creating									x	x
Masculine Powers										
Strength			x							
Courage			x							
Persistence			x							
Defender			x							
Invulnerability	x		x	x		x		x		Web
Invisibility	x					x				
Swiftness			x	x	x			x		
Observation			x	x	x	x				
Attentiveness	x		x		x	x				x
Terrifying aspects		x				x				
Power over females	x									x
Wind Powers										
Whirlwind								x	x	x
Thunder-beings			x						x	x
Confusing the enemy		x						x	x	x
Ambivalent attitudes		x			x	x				x
Metamorphosis										x
Speak Lakota							x			x
Curing Powers	x					x				
Ability to find things					x	x				
Spiritual Archetype			x			x				

Appendix D
Mammals, Birds, and Insects

The mammals which enter into Oglala subsistence and conceptualizations are here identified, where possible, with their taxonomic and Lakota names. The Lakota names followed by (S) are from Ernest Thompson Seton (*Life Histories of Northern Animals*, London, 1910); those followed by (C) are from Edward Curtis (*North American Indians*, Vol. II, 1908).

Mammals

Antelope, prong–horned	*Ta-h·cha-saⁿ-la*	(C)
	Tah-heen-cha	(S)
Badger	*Ho-ka'*	(S)
	h·o'-ka	(C)
Bat	*(hu-pá-ki-gula-ke)*	(C)
Bear, grizzly	*Ma-tó*	(C)
	Mah-tó-shah-kaý han-ská	(S)
black	*Mah-tó-wah-hay seé-cha*	
brown	*Mah-tó-hó-tah*	
Beaver	*Cham-paȟ*	(S)
	Chá-pa	(C)
Bison, bull	*Tah-tanḱ-Kah*	(S)
cow	*Pte*	(C)
Coyote	*Mee-yah-slaý-cha-lah*	(S)
	Ma shle-cha	(C)
Chipmunk	*Itayt-kaȟ-lah*	(S)
	Ta-shná-he-cha	(C)
Deer, N. White-tail	*Tah-heen-chá-lah*	(S)
mule	*Tah-hen-chá-la*	(S)
deer	*Tá-hcha*	(C)

Elk, wapiti, bull	*hay-haĥ-kah*	(S)
	he-há-ka	(C)
cow	*uⁿ-páⁿ*	(C)
Fox, Kit	*Mee-yaĥ-Chah*	(S)
	to-ká-la	(C)
Prairie Red	*Shung-ka-gélah*	(S)
	Shoⁿ-ghí-la	(C)
Goat, mountain		
Gopher, pocket	*Wah-hin-haý-ya*	(S)
Lion, mountain	*i-gūmú-taⁿ-ka*	(C)
Lynx (wildcat, bobcat)	*ig-mu-hó-ta*	(S)
	i-gūmú-gŭle-za	(C)
Martin, American sable	*Mah-ha-pah-skay-chah*	(S)
Mink, vison	*Lo-chiń-cha*	(S)
	i-ku-saⁿ	(C)
Mole		
Moose	*Tah*	(S)
	ta	(C)
Musk-rat	*Sink-pay-lah*	(S)
Otter	*Ptaⁿ*	(C)
	Ptan	(S)
Porcupine	*Pah-hiń*	(S)
Prairie dog	*Pis-piⁿ-za*	(C)

Appendix E
Oglala Personal Names
Relating to Animals or Birds

The Oglala Roster

2. Bear Looking Behind
4. White Buffalo
5. The Real Hawk
7. The Bear Stops
8. Wears the Feather
9. Dog-Eagle
10. Red Horn Bull
11. Low Dog
12. Charging Hawk
13. White Tail
16. Little Eagle
17. Spotted Skunk
18. White Bear
21. Center Feather
23. The Bear Spares Him
24. White Plume
26. Red Crow
27. The Last Bear
28. Bird Man
29. Horse-with-Horns
30. Fast Elk
32. Spotted Elk
37. Little Buffalo
43. Black Elk
46. Long-Dog
47. Iron-Hawk
48. Pretty Weasel
49. Short-Buffalo
50. Bull with Bad Heart
51. Four Crows
53. Eagle Hawk
59. Iron Crow
60. Running-Horse
61. Owns an Animal with Horns
66. Female Elk Boy
67. Little Owl
68. Pretty Horse
69. Running Eagle
71. Prairie-Chicken
73. Little Hawk
74. Standing Buffalo
75. Standing Bear
77. Bear Whirlwind
78. Sacred Cow

The Red Cloud Census

148. Spotted Horse
149. Afraid-of-Bear
150. Little-Bull
151. Red-Hawk
152. Bear-Paw
153. Eagle-Horse
154. Red-Beaver
155. Spotted-Eagle
156. Little-Crow
157. Black-Horse
158. Mouse
160. White-Eagle
162. White-Horse
165. Yellow-Horse
167. Black-Bear
169. Wolf-Stand-on-a-Hill
170. Eagle-Bear
171. Little-Wolf
172. Spotted-Elk
173. Elk-Walking-with-his-Voice
174. Weasel-Bear
175. Black-Elk
177. Poor-Bull
178. Eagle-Elk
180. Horse-Comes-Out
184. Wolf-Stands-on-Hill
185. Bear-Comes-Out
186. Good-Bull
188. Bear-that-growls
190. White-Tail
191. Feathers
193. Horned-Horse
195. Black-Bear
196. Red-War-Bonnet
197. Black-Weasel
200. Good-Bull
203. Bad-Horn
204. High-Eagle
205. Black-Bull
211. Red-Hawk
212. White-Bear

213. Many-Shells
216. Shoots-the-Animal
218. Fast-Horse
220. Yellow-Owl
221. Red-Bull
223. Black-Fox
234. Kills-the-Bear
238. High-Bear
240. Black-Bird
241. Swallow
242. Little-Elk
243. Little-Bird
244. Bear-Back
246. Buffalo-Horn
247. Iron-Bird
248. Bull
249. Eagle-Track
250. Medicine-Bird
251. Fox
252. White-Bear
253. Tall-Panther
257. Wolf
258. Black-Horse
259. White-Horse
260. Spotted-Owl
263. Big-Voiced-Eagle
264. White-Elk
265. Porcupine
268. Eagle-Feather
271. Shot-His-Horse
272. Red-Bear
274. Feather-Necklace
275. Fast-Elk
276. Black-Bull
278. Black-Deer
279. White-Cow-Man
280. Horse-the-Clothing
282. Eagle-Swallow
285. Dog-with-Good-Voice
288. Few-Tails

Notes

Introduction

Quotations

1. Frances Densmore, "Teton Sioux Music", Smithsonian Institution, Bureau of American Ethnology Bulletin (Washington, DC, 1918).
2. Charles Eastman, *Indian Boyhood* (New York: Houghton Mifflin, 1902).
3. J. O. Dorsey, *A Study of Siouan Cults*, Smithsonian Institution, Bureau of American Ethnology Annual Report (Washington, DC, 1894).
4. James Walker, "The Sun Dance and Other Ceremonies of the Oglala Division of the Teton Dakota", *American Museum of Natural History Anthropological Papers*, Vol. 16, Part 2 (New York, 1917).
5. Verne Dusenberry, "The Montana Cree", *Studies in Comparative Religion* (Stockholm, 1962).

Notes

1. Densmore, "Teton Sioux Music", 1918.
2. Edward S. Curtis, *The North American Indians*, Vol. 3 (Cambridge, Mass: The Univ. of Mass. Press, 1909).
3. Walker, Vol. 16, Part 2.
4. Clark Wissler, "The Whirlwind and the Elk in the Mythology of the Dakotas," *Journal of American Folk-Lore*, XVII (1905).
5. Ibid.

Chapter I

1. Joseph Epes Brown, "The Bison and the Moth: Lakota Correspondences," *Parabola*, Vol. 8, No. 2, 1983, p. 6.

2. A. Irving Hallowell, *Northern Saulteaux Religion Vol. 36*, 1934, pp. 392–3.
3. Joseph Epes Brown, "Modes of Contemplation Through Actions: North American Indians," *Main Currents in Modern Thought*, Vol. 30, No. 2, 1973, p. 61.
4. Ibid., pp. 61–2.
5. George Bird Grinnell, *The Cheyenne Indians of North America: Their History and Ways of Life* (Lincoln: University of Nebraska Press, 1972), p. 277.
6. Joseph Epes Brown, "Becoming Part of It," *Parabola*, Vol. 7, No. 3, 1982, p. 8.

Chapter II
1. Densmore, "Teton Sioux Music."
2. Father P. J. De Smet, *Life, Letters and Travels* (New York, 1905), p. 1016.
3. Charles A. Eastman, *Indian Boyhood* (New York: McClure, Phillips, 1902), pp. 52–56.
4. Densmore, pp. 172, 207.
5. Ibid., p. 176.
6. Ibid.
7. Clark Wissler, "Symbolism in the Decorative Art of the Sioux," *Proceedings of the International Congress of Americanists*, Vol. 13, 1902, p. 261.
8. H. H. Blish, *A Pictographic History of the Oglala Sioux* (Lincoln: University of Nebraska Press, 1967), p. 199.
9. Densmore, p. 125.
10. P. Beckwith, "Notes on the Customs of the Dakotahs," *Annual Reports Board of Regents of the Smithsonian Institution*, Washington, DC, 1926, p. 176.
11. Luther Standing Bear, "Land of the Spotted Eagle," *Stories of the Sioux* (Boston: Houghton Mifflin Co., 1934).
12. Densmore, p. 195.
13. Ibid., p. 266.
14. Ibid.
15. M. W. Beckwith, "Mythology of the Oglala Dakota," *Annual Reports Board of Regents of the Smithsonian Institution*, Vol. 43 (Washington, DC, 1930), p. 80.
16. Clark Wissler, "Societies and Ceremonial Associations in the Oglala Division of the Teton-Dakota," *Anthropological Papers of the American Museum of Natural History*, Vol. 9, Part 1, 1917, p. 31.
17. Beckwith, p. 249.

18. Dorsey, p. 496.
19. Eastman, p. 52.
20. Ibid.
21. Standing Bear, p. 15.
22. Clark Wissler, "Psychological Aspects of the Culture-Environment Relations," *American Anthropologist*, No. 2, 1912, p. 15.
23. From the author's field notes, 1949.
24. Joseph Epes Brown, *The Sacred Pipe* (Norman, Okla: University of Oklahoma Press, 1953), p. 85.
25. Louis L. Meeker, "Siouan Mythological Tales," *Journal of American Folk-Lore*, Vol. 14, 1901, p. 163.
26. Dorsey, pp. 497–8.
27. J. R. Walker, "The Sun Dance and Other Ceremonies of the Oglala Division of the Teton Dakota," *Anthropological Papers of the American Museum of Natural History*, Vol. 16, Part 2, 1917, p. 147.
28. Meeker, p. 163.
29. Royal B. Hassrick, *The Sioux: Life and Customs of a Warrior Society* (Norman, Okla: University of Oklahoma Press, 1964), p. 270.
30. Walker, p. 152.
31. Brown, *The Sacred Pipe*, p. 58.
32. From the author's field notes, winter 1949.
33. John G. Neihardt, *Black Elk Speaks* (New York: William Morrow & Co., 1932), pp. 199–200.
34. Brown, *The Sacred Pipe*, p. 6.
35. H. H. Blish, "The Ceremony of the Sacred Bow of the Oglala Dakota," *American Anthropologist*, Vol. 36, 1934, p. 185.
36. Densmore, p. 161.
37. Garrick Mallory, "Picture Writing of the North American Indians," *Bureau of American Ethnology Tenth Annual Report*, 1893, pp. 419–20.
38. Densmore, p. 181.
39. Walker, "The Sun Dance," p. 147.
40. Densmore, p. 161.
41. Ibid., p. 188.
42. Clark Wissler, "The Whirlwind and the Elk in the Mythology of the Dakotas," *Journal of American Folk-Lore*, Vol. 17, 1905, p. 259.
43. Ibid.
44. Ibid., p. 258.
45. Ibid.
46. Clark Wissler, "Decorative Art of the Sioux Indians," *Bulletins of the American Museum of Natural History*, Vol. 18, Part 3, 1904, p. 44.
47. Ibid.

Chapter III

1. Brown, "Modes of Contemplation," p. 62.
2. Brown, "Becoming Part of It," p. 11.
3. Densmore, p. 34.
4. Brown, *The Sacred Pipe*, p. 220.
5. From the author's field notes, 1949.
6. Hassrick, p. 235.
7. Densmore, p. 66.
8. Recorded by Frances Densmore from Lone Man, 1918.
9. Densmore, p. 275.
10. Brown, "Becoming Part of It," p. 11.
11. Brown, unpublished essay.
12. Ibid.
13. Wissler, "The Whirlwind and the Elk," p. 394.
14. Alice Fletcher, "The Elk Mystery of Festival," *Report of the Peabody Museum of American Archaeology and Ethnology*, Vol. 3, 1884, p. 277.
15. Clark Wissler, "General Discussion of Shamanistic and Dancing Societies," *Anthropological Papers of the American Museum of Natural History*, Vol. 11, Part 12, 1916, p. 860.
16. Dorsey, p. 477.
17. Densmore, p. 85.
18. Brown, "Becoming Part of It," p. 9.
19. Densmore, p. 97.
20. Mallory, p. 181.
21. Curtis, p. 18.
22. Wissler, "The Whirlwind and the Elk," p. 267.
23. Brown, "Becoming Part of It," p. 10.
24. Densmore, p. 104.
25. Wissler, "Societies and Ceremonial Associations," p. 54.
26. Densmore, p. 348.
27. Ibid., p. 78.
28. Brown, "Modes of Contemplation," p. 62.
29. Densmore, p. 78.
30. Densmore, p. 446.
31. Walker, p. 141.
32. Ibid., p. 122.
33. Brown, *The Sacred Pipe*, p. 114.
34. Walker, p. 98.

Chapter IV
1. Wissler, "Psychological Aspects," p. 258.

Chapter VI
1. Ivan Paulson, "The Animal Guardian: A Critical and Synthetic Review," *History of Religion*, Vol. 3, No. 2, 1963, p. 219.

Reference Bibliography

Abbreviations

AA	American Anthropologist. Washington, New York. Lancaster, Menasha
AAAPSC	The Annals of the American Academy of Political and Social Sciences
AESM	American Ethnological Society Monographs
APAM	Anthropological Papers of the American Museum of Natural History. New York
ARBAE	Annual Reports of the Bureau of American Ethnology. Washington
ARSI	Annual Reports Board of Regents of the Smithsonian Institution
BBAE	Bulletins of the Bureau of American Ethnology. Washington
BAMNH	Bulletins of the American Museum of Natural History. New York
CMAI	Contributions from the Museum of the American Indian, Heye Foundation. New York
CNAE	Contributions to North American Ethnology. Dept. of the Interior, United States Geographical and Geological Survey of the Rocky Mountain Region. Washington
EMS	Ethnographical Museum of Sweden. Stockholm
FMAS	Field Museum of Natural History. Anthropological Series. Chicago
ICA	Proceedings of the International Congress of Americanists. Paris and other cities.
JAFL	Journal of American Folk-Lore. Boston, New York
JASP	Journal of Abnormal and Social Psychology

MAA   Memoirs of the American Anthropological Society. Lancaster, Menasha

MNAS   Memoirs of the National Academy of Sciences. Washington

PMP   Peabody Museum Papers (Archaeological and Ethnological Papers of the Peabody Museum, Harvard University). Cambridge

PNAS   Proceedings of the National Academy of Sciences. Washington

PTRSC   Proceedings and Transactions of the Royal Society of Canada. Ottawa

RPM   Reports of the Peabody Museum of American Archaeology and Ethnology

RUSNM   Reports of the United States National Museum. Washington

SMC   Smithsonian (Institution) Miscellaneous Collections. Washington

SSCR   Stockholm Studies in Comparative Religion. Stockholm

UCP   University of California Publications in American Archaeology and Ethnology. Berkeley

Select Bibliography

Bates, Marston. "Human Ecology." *Anthropology Today*, ed. A. L. Kroeber (1953).

Beckwith, M. W. "Mythology of the Oglala Dakota." *Journal of American Folk-Lore*, 43 (1930).

Beckwith, P. "Notes on the Customs of the Dakotahs." *Annual Reports Board of Regents of the Smithsonian Institution* (1986).

Benedict, Ruth F. "Concept of the Guardian Spirit in North America." *Memoirs of the American Anthropological Society*, No. 29 (1932).

—— "The Vision in Plains Culture." *American Anthropologist*, 24 (1922).

Blish, H. H. "The Ceremony of the Sacred Bow of the Oglala Dakota." *American Anthropologist*, 26, No. 2 (1934).

—— "Ethical Conceptions of the Oglala Dakota." *University of Nebraska Studies*, Vol. 26 (1926).

—— *A Pictographic History of the Oglala Sioux*. Lincoln: University of Nebraska Press, 1967.

Boas, Franz, and Deloria, Ella. "Dakota Grammar." *Memoirs of the National Academy of Sciences*, Vol. 23, 2nd Memoir (1939).

Bourke, John G. "The Medicine Men of the Apache." *Annual Reports of the Bureau of American Ethnology*, No. 9 (1892).

Brown, Joseph Epes. *The Sacred Pipe*. Norman, Okla: University of Oklahoma Press, 1953.

—— *The Spiritual Legacy of the American Indian*, Pendle Hill, Haverford, (1972).

Burlingame, Merrill Gildea. "The Economic Importance of the Buffalo in the Northern Plains Region, 1800–1890." Unpublished M.A. Thesis, University of Iowa (1928).

Bushnell, D. I. "The Various Uses of Buffalo Hair by the North American Indians." *American Anthropologist*, 11 (1909).

Catlin, G. "Die Indianer und die während eines achtjähriger

Aufenthalts unter den wildesten ihrer Stämme erlebten Abenteuer und Schicksale." *Berlin-Friedenau* (1924).

Conklin, Harold. "The Relation of Hanunoo Culture to the Plant World." Unpublished. PhD Dissertation in Anthropology. New Haven, Conn: Yale University, 1954.

Curtis, Edward S. *The North American Indian: The Teton Sioux.* Cambridge, Mass: The University of Massachusetts Press, 1908.

Deloria, E. "The Sun Dance of the Oglala Sioux." *Journal of American Folk-Lore*, 42 (1929).

Denig, Edwin Thompson. "Indian Tribes of the Upper Missouri." *Annual Reports of the Bureau of American Ethnology*, 46 (1930).

Densmore, Frances. "The Belief of the Indian in a Connection between Song and the Supernatural." *Bulletins of the Bureau of American Ethnology*, No. 151. *Anthropological Papers*, No. 37 (1953).

——— "Imitative Dances among the American Indians." *Journal of American Folk-Lore*, 51 (1947).

——— "Notes on the Indian's Belief in the Friendliness of Nature." *SWJA*, 4 (1948).

——— "Technique in the Music of the American Indian." *Bulletins of the Bureau of American Ethnology*, No. 156. *Anthropological Papers*, No. 36, (1953).

——— "Teton Sioux Music." *Bulletins of the Bureau of American Ethnology*, 61 (1918).

De Smet, Father P. J. "Life, Letters and Travels." H. M. Chittendon & A. T. Richardson, Eds. (1905).

Dodge, Colonel Richard. *Our Wild Indians.* Hartford, Conn: Worthington and Company, 1883.

Dorsey, George A. "The Arapho Sun Dance." *Field Museum of Natural History*, Publ. 75, IV (1903).

Dorsey, J. O. "Osage Traditions." *Annual Reports of the Bureau of American Ethnology*, 6 (1888).

——— "Siouan Sociology." *Annual Reports of the Bureau of American Ethnology*, 15 (1897).

——— "A Study of Siouan Cults." *Annual Reports of the Bureau of American Ethnology*, 11 (1894).

——— "Teton Folklore Notes." *Journal of American Folk-Lore*, 2 (1889).

Drobin, Ulf. "Myth and Epical Motifs in the Loki-Research." *Temenos*, 3 (1968).

Dusenberry, Verne "Ceremonial Sweat Lodges of the Gros Ventre Indians." *Ethnos*, 23 (1963).

——— "The Montana Cree." *Stockholm Studies in Comparative Religion* (1962).

—— "The Significance of the Sacred Pipes to the Gros Ventre of Montana." *Ethnos*, 26 (1961).

Eastman, Charles A. *Indian Boyhood*. Boston and New York: Houghton Mifflin Co., 1902.

—— *The Soul of the Indian*. Boston: Houghton Mifflin Co., 1911.

Ewers, John C. "Early White Influence upon Plains Indian Painting." *Smithsonian (Institution) Miscellaneous Collections*, Vol. 134, No. 7 (1957).

—— "The Horse in Blackfoot Culture." *Bulletins of the Bureau of American Ethnology*, Bulletin 159 (1955).

—— *Plains Indian Painting*. Stanford, Calif: Stanford University Press, 1939.

—— "Was There a Northwestern Plains Sub-Culture?" *Plains Anthropologist*, Vol. 12, No. 36 (1967).

Feraca, Stephen E. "The Yuwipi Cult of the Oglala." *Plains Anthropologist*, Vol. 5, No. 13 (1961).

Fernberger and Speck, F. "Two Sioux Shields and Their Psychological Interpretation." *Journal of Abnormal and Social Psychology*, Vol. 33, No. 2 (1938).

Fletcher, Alice C. "The Elk Mystery of Festival." *Reports of the Peabody Museum of American Archaeology and Ethnology*, XVI-XVII (1883).

—— "The Hako: A Pawenee Ceremony." *Annual Reports of the Bureau of American Ethnology*, Vol. 22 (1904).

—— "Indian and Nature." *American Anthropologist* (1907).

—— "The Religious Ceremony of the Four Winds or Quarters." *Reports of the Peabody Museum of American Archaeology and Ethnology*, 3(b) (1884).

—— "The Shadow or Ghost Lodge: A Ceremony of the Oglala Sioux." *Reports of the Peabody Museum of American Archaeology and Ethnology*, 16th and 17th Annual Report 25, Vol. III, Nos. 3 and 4 (1884).

—— "The 'Wawan' or Pipe Dance of the Omahas." *Peabody Museum Papers*, Vol. III, Nos. 3 and 4 (1884).

Fletcher, C. and La Flesche, F. "The Omaha Tribe." *Annual Reports of the Bureau of American Ethnology*, 27 (1906).

Forde, C. Daryll. *Habitat, Economy and Society: A Geographical Introduction to Ethnology*, London, 1949.

Frake, Charles O. "Cultural Ecology and Ethnography." *American Anthropologist*, 64:1 (1962).

—— "The Ethnographic Study of Cognitive Systems in *Anthropology and Human Behaviour*. Gladwin and Sturtevant, eds. (1962).

Gilmore, Melvin R. "Some Cosmogonic Ideas of the Dakotas." *American Anthropologist*, 28 (1926).

Granlund, John "Birdskin Caps." *Ethnos*, 18 (1953).

Grinnell, G. P. *Blackfoot Lodge Tales*. New York: Charles Scribner's Sons, 1920.

—— "A Buffalo Sweatlodge." *American Anthropologist*, 21 (1919).

—— "Butterfly and Spider among the Blackfoot." *American Anthropologist*, 1 (1899).

—— *The Cheyenne Indians*, Vols. I and II. New Haven, Conn: Yale University Press, 1923.

—— "Great Mysteries of the Cheyenne." *American Anthropologist*, 12 (1910).

—— *Pawnee, Blackfoot and Cheyenne*. New York: Charles Scribner's Sons, 1961.

Gudger, E. W. "Spiders as Fisherman and Hunters." *Natural History*, Vol. XXV, No. 3 (1925).

Haekel, Joseph. Der "Herr der Tiere" in Glauben der Indianer Mesoamerikas. Hamburg. Amerikanistische Miszellen-Mitteilungen aus dem Museum für Volkerkunde, XXV (1959).

Haines, F. "The Northward Spread of Horses Among the Plains Indians." *American Anthropologist*, 40, Nos. 2 and 3 (1938).

Hallowell, A. Irving "Bear Ceremonialism in the Northern Hemisphere." *American Anthropologist*, 28 (1926).

—— *Culture and Experience*. Philadelphia: University of Pennsylvania Press, 1955.

—— *Northern Saulteaux Religion*, No. 36 (1934).

—— *Ojibwa Metaphysics of Being*. Ragiuri, R. and Petrullo L. (eds.), Stanford, Calif: Stanford University Press, 1958.

—— "Ojibwa Ontology, Behaviour and World View." *Culture in History*. Essays in Honor of Paul Radin (1960).

Harrington, J. P. and Henderson, J. "Ethno-zoology of the Tewa Indians." *Bulletins of the Bureau of American Ethnology*, 56 (1914).

Hassrick, Royal E. *The Sioux: Life and Customs of a Warrior Society*. Norman, Okla: University of Oklahoma Press, 1964.

—— "Teton Dakota Kinship System," *American Anthropologist*, 56, No. 3 (1944).

Hewitt, J. N. B. "Handbook of American Indians." *Bulletins of the Bureau of American Ethnology*, 30, Part 1 (1907).

Hoebel, Wallace "The Political Organizaton and Life-Ways of the Comanche Indians." *Memoirs of the American · Anthropological Society*, 54 (1950).

Hornaday, William T. "The Extermination of the American Bison." *Reports of the United States National Museum* (1889).

Howard, James H. "Yanktonai Dakota Eagle Trapping." *SWJA*, 10 (1954).

Hultkrantz, Åke "Conceptions of the Soul Among North American Indians." *Ethnographical Museum of Sweden*, Monograph Series, 1 (1953).

—— "Configurations of Religious Belief among the Wind River Shoshoni." *Ethnos*, 21 (1956).

—— "An Ecological Approach to Religion." *Ethnos*, 31 (1966).

—— "The Indians and the Wonders of the Yellowstone." *Ethnos*, 19 (1954).

—— "The Mastery of the Animals Among the Wind River Shoshoni." *Ethnos*, 4 (1961).

—— "The North American Indian Orpheus Tradition." Monograph Series 2. *Ethnographical Museum of Sweden* (1957).

—— "The Origin of Death Myth as Found Among the Wind River Shashoni Indians.," *Ethnos*, 20 (1955).

—— "Les Religions des Indiens Primitifs de l'Amerique." *Stockholm Studies in Comparative Religion* (1963).

—— "Shoshoni Indians on the Plains: An Appraisal of the Documentary Evidence." *Zeitschrift für Ethnologie Band 93*, Heft 1. 2 (1968).

—— "The Supernatural Owners of Nature." *Stockholm Studies in Comparative Religion* (1960).

—— "Type of Religion in the Arctic Hunting Cultures." *Hunting and Fishing*. Luleå : Norrbottens Museum (1965).

Humphrey, Norman D. "A Characterization of Certain Plains Associations." *American Anthropologist*, 43 (1941).

Hurt, Wesley R. "A Yuwipi Ceremony at Pine Ridge." *Plains Anthropologist*, Vol. 5, No. 10 (1960).

James, E. O. "Tutelary Gods and Spirits." *Encyclopaedia of Religion and Ethics* (1921).

Jenness, Diamond. "The Indian's Interpretation of Man and Nature." *Proceedings and Transactions of the Royal Society of Canada*, 3rd Ser. XXIV, Section II (1930).

Jones, William. "The Algonkin Manitou." *Journal of American Folk-Lore*, 15 (1905).

Kock, Gösta. "Is 'Der Heilbringer' a God or Not?" *Ethnos*, 8 (1943).

La Flesche, Francis. "Who Was the Medicine Man?" *Journal of American Folk-Lore*, 18 (1905).

Lee, Dorothy. *Freedom and Culture*. New York: A Spectrum Book, 1959.

Lesser, Alexander. "Some Aspects of Siouan Kinship." *Proceedings of the International Congress of Americanists*, XXIII (1928).

Levi-Strauss, Claude. *The Savage Mind*. Chicago: University of Chicago Press, 1966.

Linderman, Frank Bird. *American: The Life Story of a Great Indian, Plenty-coups, Chief of the Crows.* New York: John Day Co., 1930.

Linton, Ralph. *The Study of Man: An Introduction.* New York: Appleton–Century, 1936.

Lowie, Robert H. *Indian Theologians.* Santa Fe: El Placio, 1933.

—— *Indians of the Plains.* New York: McGraw-Hill, 1954.

—— *Primitive Religion.* Boni & Liveright, 1924.

—— "Religion in Human Life." *American Anthropologist*, 65 (1963).

—— "Studies in Plains Indian Folklore." *University of California Publications in American Archaeology and Ethnology*, Vol. 40, No. 1 (1942).

Lyford, Carrie A. "Quill and Beadword of the Western Sioux." *Bureau of Indian Affairs* (1940).

McAllester, David. "Frances Densmore and American Indian Music." *American Anthropologist*, 72, No. 1 (1970).

McClintock, Walter. *The Old North Trail.* London: The Macmillan Co. 1910.

McGee, W. J. "Ponca Feather Symbolism." *American Anthropologist*, 11 (1898).

Mallory, Garrick. "Pictographs of the American Indian." *Annual Reports of the Bureau of American Ethnology*, No. 11 (1886).

—— *Picture-writing of the American Indians.* New York: Dover Publications, 1972.

Meeker, Louis L. "Siouan Mythological Tales." *Journal of American Folk-Lore*, 14 (1901).

Mishkin, Bernard. "Rank and Warfare Among the Plains Indians." *American Ethnological Society Monographs*, No. 3 (1948).

Mooney, James. *The Ghost-Dance Religion and Wounded Knee*, 2 vols. New York: Dover Publications, 1973.

Murdock, George Peter. "Ethnographic Bibliography of North America." *Human Relations Area Files* (1960).

Neihardt, John G. *Black Elk Speaks: Being the Life Story of a Holy Man of the Oglala Sioux.* New York: Washington Square Press, 1959.

Nelson, Richard K. "Make Prayers to the Raven, a Koyukon View of the Northern Forest." Chicago: The University of Chicago Press, (1983).

Paulson, Ivar. "The Animal Guardian: A Critical and Synthetic Review." *History of Religion*, Vol. 3:2 (1963).

—— "Le rapport des ames animals avec les etres gardiens dans les croyances religieuses des peuples Siberiens." *Ethnos*, 25 (1960).

—— "Schutzgeister und Gottheiten des Weldes. (Der Jagdfiere und Fische)" *Nordeurasien. Stockholm Studies in Comparative Religion* (1961).

Powell, J. H. "Indian Linguistic Families of America North of Mexico." *Annual Reports of the Bureau of American Ethnology*, No. 7 (1891).

Preuss, K. "Monumentale vorgeschichtliche Kunst," Vols. I–II. *Göttingen* (1929).

Radin, Paul. "Religion of the North American Indians." *Journal of American Folk-Lore*, 27 (1914).

Riggs, Stephen R. "Grammar and Dictionary of the Dakota Language." *SCK*, No. IV (1852).

Rydén, Stig. "A Seventeenth Century Indian Headdress from Delaware." *Ethnos*, 28 (1963).

Sanders, William T. "Cultural Ecology in Nuclear Mesoamerica." *American Anthropologists* 64 (1962).

Seton, Ernest Thompson. *Life-Histories of Northern Animals: An Account of the Mammals of Manitoba*, 2 vols. New York: C. Scribner's Sons, 1909.

Smith, J. L. A Ceremony of the Preparation of the Offering Cloths for Presentation to the Sacred Calf Pipe of the Teton Sioux." *Plains Anthropologist*, Vol. 9, No. 25 (1964).

Speck, Frank and Hassrick, Royal. "A Plains Indian Shield and Its Interpretation." *Primitive Man*, Vol. 21, Nos. 3 and 4 (1948).

Spier, Leslie. "The Association Test as a Method of Defining Religious Conceptions." *AANS*, 29 (1927).

Standing Bear, Luther. "Land of the Spotted Eagle." *Stories of the Sioux*. Boston: Houghton Mifflin Co. 1934.

Thomas, N. W. "Origin and Concepts Relating to Animals." *Hastings Encyclopedia of Religion and Ethics*, 1 (1921).

Thomas, Sidney J. "A Sioux Medicine Bundle." *American Anthropologist*, 43 (1941).

Thomson, Stith. *Tales of the North American Indians*. Cambridge: Harvard University Press, 1929.

Tilghman, Z. A. "Source of the Buffalo Origin Legend." *American Anthropologist*, 53 (1941).

Underhill, Ruth Murray. "Religion Among American Indians." *The Annals of the American Academy of Political and Social Sciences*, 311 (1957).

Voget, Fred W. "Warfare in the Integration of Crow Culture." *Explorations in Cultural Anthropology*. New York: McGraw-Hill Book Co., 1964.

Walker, J. R. "The Sun Dance and Other Ceremonies of the Oglala Division of the Teton Dakota." *Anthropological Papers of the American Museum of Natural History*, XVI, Part II (1917).

Wallis, Wilson D. "Beliefs and Tales of the Canadian Dakotas." *Journal of American Folk-Lore*, 36 (1923).

Weygold, Freiderich von. "Das Indianische Lederzelt im Königlichen Museum für Volkerkunde zu Berlin." *Globus. Sonder-Abdruck Band*, LXXXIII, No. 1 (1903).

Wildschut, William. "Crow Indian Medicine Bundles." *Contributions from the Museum of the American Indian*, XVII (1960).

Wilson, H. C. "An Inquiry into the Nature of Plains Cultural Development." *American Anthropologist*, 65:2 (1963).

Wissler, Clark. *The American Indian: An Introduction to the Anthropology of the New World*. Gloucester, Mass: P. Smith, 1957.

———— "Decorative Art of the Sioux Indians." *Bulletins of the Bureau of American Ethnology*, 18, Part 3 (1904).

———— "General Discussion of Shamanistic and Dancing Societies." *Anthropological Papers of the American Museum of Natural History*, XI, Part XII (1916).

———— "The Influence of the Horse in the Development of Plains Culture." *American Anthropologist*, 16 (1914).

———— "Psychological Aspects of the Culture-Environment Relation." *American Anthropologist*, 14:2 (1912).

———— "Societies and Ceremonial Associations in the Oglala Division of the Teton-Dakota." *Anthropological Papers of the American Museum of Natural History*, XI, Part 1 (1912).

———— "Some Dakota Myths." *Journal of American Folk-Lore*, 20, LXXVI (1907).

———— "Some Protective Designs of the Dakota." *Anthropological Papers of the American Museum of Natural History*, 1, Part 2 (1907).

———— "Symbolism in the Decorative Art of the Sioux." *Proceedings of the International Congress of Americanists*, XIII (1902).

———— "The Whirlwind and the Elk in the Mythology of the Dakotas." *Journal of American Folk-Lore*, 17 (1905).

Zerries, Otto. "Wild und Buschgeister in Südamerika." *Studien zur Kulturkunde*, XI (1954).

———— "Wildgeister und Jagdritual in Zentralamerika." *Amerikanistische Miszellen-Mitteilungen aus dem Museum für Volkkunde*, XXV (1959).